INCLUSIVE
CONVERSATIONS

Fostering Equity, Empathy,
and Belonging across Differences

INCLUSIVE
CONVERSATIONS

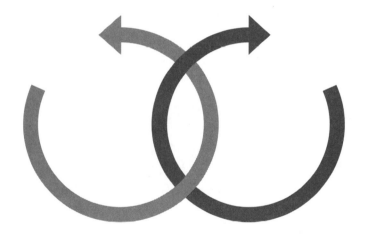

MARY-FRANCES WINTERS

BK

Berrett–Koehler Publishers, Inc.

Berrett-Koehler Publishers, Inc.
1333 Broadway, Suite 1000, Oakland, CA 94612-1921
Tel: (510) 817-2277 / Fax: (510) 817-2278
www.bkconnection.com

ORDERING INFORMATION

QUANTITY SALES. Special discounts are available on quantity purchases by corporations, associations, and others. For details, contact the "Special Sales Department" at the Berrett-Koehler address above.

INDIVIDUAL SALES. Berrett-Koehler publications are available through most bookstores. They can also be ordered directly from Berrett-Koehler: Tel: (800) 929-2929; Fax: (802) 864-7626; www.bkconnection.com.

ORDERS FOR COLLEGE TEXTBOOK/COURSE ADOPTION USE. Please contact Berrett-Koehler: Tel: (800) 929-2929; Fax: (802) 864-7626.

Distributed to the US trade and internationally by Penguin Random House Publisher Services.

Berrett-Koehler and the BK logo are registered trademarks of Berrett-Koehler Publishers, Inc.

Printed in the United States.

Berrett-Koehler books are printed on long-lasting acid-free paper. When it is available, we choose paper that has been manufactured by environmentally responsible processes. These may include using trees grown in sustainable forests, incorporating recycled paper, minimizing chlorine in bleaching, or recycling the energy produced at the paper mill.

Library of Congress Cataloging-in-Publication Data

Names: Winters, Mary-Frances, author.
Title: Inclusive conversations : fostering equity, empathy, and belonging across differences / Mary-Frances Winters.
Description: First edition. | Oakland, CA : Berrett-Koehler Publishers, [2020] | Includes bibliographical references and index. Identifiers: LCCN 2020008984 | ISBN 9781523088805 (paperback) | ISBN 9781523088812 (pdf) | ISBN 9781523088829 (epub)
Subjects: LCSH: Communication in organizations. | Interpersonal communication. | Conversation. | Interpersonal conflict. Classification: LCC HD30.3 .W555 2020 | DDC 302.3/5—dc23. LC record available at https://lccn.loc.gov/2020008984

FIRST EDITION

28 27 26 25 24 23 22 21 20 || 10 9 8 7 6 5 4 3 2 1

Book producer and text design and compostion: BookMatters; Cover designer: Rob Johnson, Toprotype Inc.; Copyeditor: Amy Smith Bell; Proofer: Janet Reed Blake; Indexer: Leonard Rosenbaum

To the generations of freedom fighters, civil rights leaders, and social justice advocates who preceded me in the ongoing quest for an inclusive, equitable world that values the dignity of all people.

And especially to those, past and present, who have lost their lives in the struggle.

CONTENTS

PREFACE

The 2020 coronavirus pandemic has put a spotlight on the stark differences in socioeconomic standing that we as a global society face and how it disproportionately impacts different groups of around the world. Inclusive conversations are sorely needed if we, as humans, are going to figure out how to share the planet in ways that foster peace and mutual understanding rather than hate, polarization, and divisiveness. There is increasing evidence in all sectors—from politics to the workplace—that we are not doing a very good job with the former and the latter is becoming a way of life. More and more, our way of communicating about racial, ethnic, gender, religious, gender identity, socio-economic, and political differences is contentious and filled with derogatory personal attacks. When we disagree on matters big or small, we dig in deep defending our own positions, denigrating those who may have a different belief. This polarizing way of communication is all too prevalent in social media spaces, where personal attacks proliferate, and it is rare to see evidence of inclusive conversations. This became evident during the coronavirus outbreak, with people even taking up arms to protest decisions that states made about the length of time social distancing would stay in effect.

Our inability to engage in inclusive conversations can fuel violence in the workplace, in schools, on the streets, and in places of worship. The increasing global climate of acrimony seeps into our everyday lives in ways that we may not even realize. It can impact personal and workplace relationships, our sense of safety, and our ability to trust each other. Inclusive conversations are needed to build and restore our connectedness as humans, to kindle respect for the dignity of every individual, and ultimately to lead to better outcomes for historically marginalized groups.

From engaging in routine performance discussions in the workplace across dimensions of diversity to talking with children about differences, we often struggle to find the right words. In my work as a diversity, equity, inclusion (DEI) consultant, I regularly witness these struggles. It is not that most people do not want to engage in inclusive conversations; they do not know how. They do not know what to say so as not to offend or be accused of insensitivity or worse. In today's divisive climate we may be afraid to offer our perspective fearing that it might spark a verbal attack.

In 2017, I wrote *We Can't Talk about That at Work: How to Talk about Race, Religion and Politics and Other Polarizing Topics* to provide a road map for the prerequisites for engaging in conversations on what are often divisive subjects. *Inclusive Conversations: Fostering Equity, Empathy, and Belonging across Differences* goes deeper to lay out the conditions for effectively engaging in dialogue that fosters equity, empathy, and belonging, not only in the workplace but also in other settings. The book chronicles both the challenges and the solutions in creating and sustaining these conditions

I have learned from consulting with many organizations over the years that the ability to have difficult conversations effectively across difference is more about creating the right conditions than having a list of dos and don'ts about what to say (and not say). We have to go deeper in understanding why we should and should not say certain things across diversity dimensions. We need to have a more fundamental understanding of the historical inequities disproportionately suffered by some groups, many of which persist today. We have to create organizational cultures that are equitable, trusting, empathetic, accepting, forgiving, inclusive, and willing to acknowledge and address power dynamics. Inclusive conversations are not easy, but they are much more likely to be fruitful when these conditions are met. Most organizations strive to be all of these things. They have values and purpose statements, principles and guidelines that purport to create equitable and inclusive environments. The problem is too many of us have opposite experiences of inequitable, unaccepting, mistrusting environments, and inclusive conversations cannot happen under these conditions.

Inclusive Conversations provides practical guidance for engaging in inclusive conversations while elucidating the layers of complexities involved. The book is written for those who have historically found themselves in dominant, power positions as well as those who have historically been subordinated and marginalized because of their identity including race, ethnicity, gender, religion, sexual orientation, or other dimension of difference. Terms such as "dominant," "subordinated," "marginalized," and others that may not be familiar to all readers are **highlighted** in the text and defined within the main text, as well as in a comprehensive glossary in the back of the book. If you lead a team or are a member of a team at work; if you are an educator, a religious leader, a politician, or a volunteer; if you are in any environment where different identities and cultures come together, this book can help you have more effective and inclusive conversations—a prerequisite for dismantling inequitable systems.

I Don't Know What to Say

I recently consulted with a large technology company on how to effectively engage in Bold, Inclusive Conversations. Based on topics I explore in *We Can't Talk about That at Work: How to Talk about Race, Religion and Politics and Other Polarizing Topics,* one of the participants, a leader in the organization, asked how he might have handled a difficult situation in the moment. This company is very progressive in advancing diversity, equity, and inclusion and routinely offers structured opportunities for employees to share their unique experiences, to tell their stories. To demonstrate vulnerability, one of the company's values, this leader shared a story about a time when he made a mistake when referring to someone in the LGBTQ community. He used the wrong terminology, which upset the employee. His purpose for sharing this situation was to illustrate that we will make mistakes, but we can recover from them if we are willing to acknowledge our mistakes and learn from them.

As this leader was sharing the story, several in the audience of about three hundred were snickering and laughing. Although he was not sure what sparked the laughter, it made him feel very uncomfortable. He thought perhaps the laughter was targeted at the particular reference to the LGBTQ community because it seemed to start at the point where he named the mistake. What should he do? Address the situation in real time, or wait until after the session and reach out to those who were laughing? If he chooses to address it immediately, what should he say? If he does not address it immediately, what will other participants think? If he addresses it immediately, will he embarrass the "perpetrators"? I share my perspective on this example in Chapter 4.

At another site conducting a similar session on Bold, Inclusive Conversations, a client asked, "What do I do when people accuse me of being too sensitive when I bring up something I feel is inappropriate?" For example, it is common in this organization for people to use the phrase "you guys" generically across gender identities. I admit that I am guilty of using that phrase pretty indiscriminately as well, so when a participant brought it up, it gave me pause. This participant wanted to know if there are boundaries to inclusion, and if we are just moving to an environment of extreme political correctness where anything you say might be interpreted as racist, sexist, homophobic, or xenophobic. Is this the world we really want to live in? The client asked, "How do we talk about this?" I share my answer in Chapter 11.

In yet another situation, the client brought The Winters Group in because they were hearing rumblings from white male employees who had been with the company for a number of years that they did not feel relevant anymore. "If you are not a woman, a person of color, or from the LGBTQ community," as the sentiment was described, "you don't seem to matter much anymore." How do we ensure that everybody feels like they belong? How do we talk about this? Read my ideas in Chapter 10.

In a cultural proficiency session with teachers in a public school system, one of the participants shared her belief that Black parents do not care as much about their children's education. Another participant vehemently disagreed and an uncomfortable conversation ensued. What should the facilitator do to turn the conversation into an effective learning experience that maintains the dignity of all involved? I discuss this issue in Chapter 7.

In each of these scenarios the questions are the same: How *do* we have meaningful conversations across difference? How do we know the "right" things to say? Conversations about any challenging, controversial topic are not easy, and conversations about topics that deal with dimensions of diversity are even harder and require a different skillset. Leaders, employees, educators, and students all need to learn how to dialogue across difference to achieve organizational goals. Many organizations—both in the corporate and not-for-profit sectors—have been intentional in creating more processes for structured dialogue about such topics as race, gender, gender identity, religion, and other dimensions of difference. They recognize this as a key ingredient in fostering a culture of inclusion and belonging, allowing them to reap measurable benefits such as increased equity, innovation, and retention. *Inclusive Conversations* helps you effectively address dilemmas like the ones posed above and more. The book also provides you with a deeper understanding of the underlying social psychology of why these types of conversations can be so challenging.

⊣ ONE ⊢

What Are Inclusive Conversations and Why Are They Important?

In today's increasingly polarized world, developing the capability for inclusive conversations is imperative. If we hope to effectively address our differences and move forward as a society with a shared vision for equity and inclusion. We have to learn how to have meaningful discourse with each other.

What Are Inclusive Conversations?

Inclusive conversations are dialogues between two or more people of different cultural backgrounds (e.g., race, ethnicity, religion, **gender, gender identity,** ability status, class/socioeconomic, or other dimension of difference) attempting to achieve an equitable outcome. Inclusive conversations consider power dynamics and **systems of inequity.** Inclusive conversations require the courage to critically self-reflect, to acknowledge what you don't know, and to embrace a willingness to learn. The desired outcome of inclusive conversations is enhanced mutual understanding that leads to equitable solutions.

Why Do We Need to Have Inclusive Conversations?

Inclusive conversations are needed to enhance cross-difference understanding so that we can address the widening divide across racial, gender, religious, socioeconomic status, and gender identity lines. At the extreme, we are witnessing an increase in hate crimes and violence, and in everyday encounters we see growing inequities in our schools, workplaces, and political and religious spheres. We are experiencing a level of polarization like no other in modern time. Conversations are becoming less civil, more hate-filled, and consequently society is making little progress in resolving our differences and achieving inclusion.

Incivility and hateful rhetoric regularly play out in social media feeds, where verbal attacks are common. In face-to-face settings we are more apt not to talk at all about potentially polarizing topics. When we do, the conversations are either contentious or shallow; either way, we are stuck. If we don't learn to talk about our differences, there is no hope for achieving **equity**, **inclusion**, and **belonging**.

Why in the Workplace?

The workplace is a microcosm of larger society. Many people spend more time at work than they do in other life pursuits. Research shows that during a typical fifty-year stint of employment, most people spend 25 percent of their waking hours working. Therefore the workplace can have a substantial influence on shaping the broader society as a site where understanding, kindness, compassion, inclusion, and empathy are the norm, rather than incivility, hate, violence, and a whole string of "isms," including racism, sexism, ageism, heterosexism, and other forms of discrimination.

The workplace struggles to hold inclusive conversations. A recent study from the Society for Human Resource Management on toxic workplaces reported that nearly four in ten working Americans say their manager fails to frequently engage in honest conversations about work topics. Similarly, one in five Americans are uncomfortable engaging in such conversations with their manager. The report goes on to say that toxicity is rampant in the workplace and often plays out as sexual harassment and discrimination.[1] The lack of effective conversations impacts employee retention and productivity. The discomfort and inability to effectively interact across difference impacts performance and career conversations (e.g., who gets selected for special assignments).

As a result of the recent attention on sexual harassment from the #MeToo movement, 60 percent of men say they are afraid of mentoring, socializing, or being alone with women at work.[2] According to research by McKinsey and LeanIn.org, women of color are less supported by their white leaders, which has contributed to their inability to move up the corporate ladder. Their bosses are less likely to promote their work contributions to others, help them navigate organizational politics, or socialize outside of work as they do with their white direct reports. These outcomes for women, and women of color specifically, will continue if we do not find ways to have inclusive conversations in the workplace.[3]

Even though some employees may be uncomfortable talking with their managers, they are increasingly willing to stage protests for what they feel is unfair treatment. According to a recent article in an HR magazine, employees aren't afraid to challenge their employers on workplace and social issues.[4] For example, in 2018 more than twenty thousand Google employees participated in a walkout to protest the handling of a sexual harassment claim where the alleged perpetrator was granted a large payout to leave. In 2019 some employees planned a sit-in to protest alleged retaliation against those who had participated in the walkout.[5] In 2019 the furniture and home goods retailer Wayfair came under fire after press reports revealed that they had sold beds to furnish migrant detention centers. Employees organized walkouts to protest the sales.[6] These protests illustrate what experts see as a cultural shift in the workplace fueled by **millennial** workers. Without effective ways to engage in inclusive conversations, such protests are likely to become commonplace.

Why with Children?

It is important to start having inclusive conversations with children to enhance their self-concept and their ability to value and respect differences. Starting young can improve children's ability to eventually enter the workplace with a greater capacity to engage in inclusive conversations. However, according to research released in 2019, most parents hardly ever discuss race/ethnicity, gender, class, or other categories of **social identity** with their children. The survey of more than six thousand parents conducted by Sesame Workshop and National Opinion Research Center (NORC) at the University of Chicago, found that the fact that parents are not discussing these issues with their kids is a real concern because children are hardwired to notice differences at a young age and ask questions.[7] Even parents who responded that they are comfortable talking about **diversity** topics such as **race** and sexual orientation admitted that they do not. If we leave children alone to make sense of differences that they see with only stereotypical references from media as their source for understanding, children may enter the workforce continuing to perpetuate the discomfort and lack of skill in engaging in inclusive conversations.

Why with Religion?

With the increase of different religions in the global workplace and the rise of religious violence, it is important for us to learn how to have inclusive conversations about religion. According to Pew Research, more than 50 percent of respondents said that they do not discuss religion even with family.[8] Learning to engage in inclusive conversations about religion can enhance cross-cultural understanding and create more inclusive work environments as well. Understanding the various practices of your co-workers can increase the likelihood that you will not make embarrassing mistakes and that you can take others' practices into account when planning workplace activities.

We continue to witness increased religious intolerance globally, with violence against Jewish synagogues on the rise. Violent crimes against Jews in the United States doubled in 2018, according to the Anti-Defamation League's annual audit of anti-Semitic incidents.[9] Of course, the most notable of these in the United States was the mass killing of eleven Jewish worshippers at the Tree of Life Synagogue in Pittsburgh in 2018. There continues to be violence against Muslims around the world, including the 2018 attack in New Zealand, killing fifty-one. Muslims in the United States report having high levels of anxiety and fear.[10]

Within Christianity there is polarization around such issues as sexual orientation. The United Methodist Church, the largest protestant denomination in the United States, voted in 2019 by a narrow margin (53 percent to 47 percent) to keep the "traditional plan" of not allowing clergy to perform same-sex marriage or ordain noncelibate gay pastors.[11] These events may be triggering and may cause trauma for students and employees, which impacts their ability to do their best work. Learning how to respond when these unfortunate events occur is key to creating inclusive environments and enhancing sense of belonging.

Why with Politics?

Politics has always been an off-limits topic, especially in the workplace. While political discussions may still be best avoided at work, it is increasingly difficult not to have politics come up in conversation. For example, a global company may have to deal with restrictions on employees being able to easily enter certain countries or even come back into a country where they reside due to restrictive immigration policies. For example, the 2019 protests in Hong Kong about democracy and political independence from mainland China sparked extreme political polarization and violence. The Winters Group was asked to support developing training for employees of multinational companies to develop skills to engage in conversations where co-workers may have different political ideologies.

Right-wing conservative political ideologies are gaining in popularity as evidenced by who is getting elected around the world. Nationalism has always been a feature across Europe's political spectrum, but there has been a recent boom in voter support for right-wing and populist parties in countries like

Austria, the Czech Republic, Germany, Hungary, Italy, and Spain. Of course, with the current administration in the United States, there are strong anti-immigrant policies and practices. While "right wing" does not necessarily mean anti-inclusion, the characteristics typically include nationalism and **ethnocentrism**, and "far right wing" often means anti-immigration and anti-integration stances toward groups that such ideologies often deem inferior and undesirable. The capacity to discuss political differences and advocate for equity for all will increasingly be a necessary skill.

Why with Social Media

Political conversations and discussions about diversity topics such as race are rampant on social media feeds, where the discourse is often hate-filled. Social media will continue to be a prime venue in the foreseeable future for sharing different perspectives, and we can either learn how to do so in constructive ways that foster understanding and learning or continue the unproductive use as a tool to proliferate hate and the "cancel culture" (discussed in Chapter 7).

The Winters Group conducted a virtual learning lab in late 2019 focused on the future of diversity, equity, and inclusion (DEI) work called "What Lies Ahead." We polled the approximately 150 participants with this question: Do you think social media will continue to foster polarization and hate in the future, or will it be an enabler for inclusive conversations and learning? Two-thirds of participants responded that social media would continue to fuel hate. I was really disheartened by that response but perhaps not surprised. We need to learn how to have inclusive conversations on social media or suffer the consequences:

extremes can and do lead to violence. I discuss strategies for inclusive conversations on social media in Chapter 11.

Why for Other Aspects of Society?

The inability to effectively talk about, understand, and address our differences leads to the proliferation of segregated neighborhoods, unfair criminal justice systems, health-care disparities, serious wealth gaps, inequitable education, violence against women and other identities, and the list goes on. To ameliorate the vast inequities that continue to persist, conversations about social injustices need to address the systems that perpetuate them. If we can't even effectively talk about society's problems, how can we hope to go deeper to dismantle the root causes? Many conversations about solutions to our social problems recommend Band-Aid fixes that do not address the underlying system. It is hard to even understand the systems because they are so interconnected, entrenched, and insidious. Learning how to dialogue about systems and then take a systems approach to these issues is the only way we can hope to eradicate inequities in our workplaces, our schools, and society in general.

Inclusive Conversations Yield Positive Workplace Results

While social justice advocates primarily in the not-for-profit world have encouraged and taught skills for dialogue on race and other social identity topics for some time, this type of dialogue is fairly new to the corporate arena. Corporate leaders are finding that developing structured opportunities for such conversation is good for business and can actually lead to greater productivity, engagement, innovation, and retention among employees.

Tim Ryan, CEO of PricewaterhouseCooper (PwC), conceived the CEO Action for Diversity and Inclusion Initiative, a consortium of more than 450 organizations, which declared a Day of Understanding on December 7, 2018, for member organizations to hold formal discussions about race. On the heels of one of PwC's **Black** employees, Botham Jean, being killed by an off-duty police officer in Dallas (she entered his apartment thinking it was hers and shot Jean), Ryan beckoned his fellow CEOs to use the opportunity to engage in dialogue to foster greater understanding. That day, 150 organizations heeded the call using a variety of conversation methods to talk about race, including panel discussions, town hall–type meetings, and outside speakers. Ryan said, to put it simply, "if we listen and understand each other better as human beings, we'll do things differently."[12] The Winters Group supported several organizations that responded to Ryan's call. The Day of Understanding is now an annual event among participating organizations.

The Winters Group conducts a three-day Train the Trainer session based on the principles in *We Can't Talk about That at Work* to equip organizations with skilled facilitators to conduct conversations. Companies and public entities such as Merck, UnitedHealthcare, Shell Oil Company, Alaska Airlines, MassMutual, and the State of Minnesota, among many other organizations, have received certification in Engaging in Bold, Inclusive Conversations. Other organizations are developing models and spaces for identity-based dialogues. For example, Progressive insurance used the principles in *We Can't Talk about That at Work* to develop a series of dialogues initially around race that have been so successful that other topics (such a LGBTQ, disabilities, and age) have been added. Called Courageous Conversations, these interactions are designed to create space for growth, sharing, and learning as it relates to dimensions of difference through a variety of lenses. Courageous Conversations leverage short case studies about the real-life experiences of people from various backgrounds to spark dialogue.

Sodexo, the food services and facilities management company, has used the principles in *We Can't Talk about That at Work* to develop learning experiences for its Business Resource Groups (BRG) around authentic dialogue. The Winters Group has supported the design of a Train the Trainer curriculum to equip BRG leaders in facilitating authentic conversations. In addition, The Winters Group has codesigned a dialogue series that focuses specifically on race, religion, and politics. Merck has also embraced the Engaging in Bold, Inclusive Conversations model and is successfully conducting sessions across the company teaching the principles of effective cross-cultural dialogue.

Since 2016 a large professional services consulting firm has retained The Winters Group to design and conduct several dialogue sessions around the country to address external events that have incited fear and anxiety among their employees. Many employees at the firm work remotely at client sites, and this is an opportunity to provide a **brave space** to share experiences and concerns particularly in light of the current sociopolitical climate in the United States. Through inclusive conversations, the goal is to create safe and trusting spaces for employees to have complex, and sometimes difficult, discussions about diversity and inclusion topics. The sessions seek to bring employees from all backgrounds to listen and act with empathy and build trust.

At the beginning of each session we conduct a live poll asking for one word that captured how they felt about the current sociopolitical climate. The responses include "exasperated," "concerned," "helpless," "fatigued," "frustrated," "polarized," "unsettled," "open-minded," and "dismayed." A few had more positive responses like "curious," "optimistic," and "blessed." By the end of the sessions the responses are much more positive, including such words as "encouraged," "educated," "knowledgeable," "optimistic," and "equipped." Many employees shared that it was cathartic to be given the opportunity to discuss their feelings, to be affirmed by colleagues, and to have some tips for engaging in inclusive conversations about polarizing topics.

In an interview, Michele Meyer-Shipp, chief diversity officer at KPMG, shared that as a result of very successful dialogue sessions across the company's footprint on the Day of Understanding in 2018, they have continued dialogue sessions with the "Talking Inclusion Series," which focuses on specific topics of interest that surfaced in a survey KPMG conducted. Employee input was consistent in their acknowledgment that "we don't know what we don't know, and we want to be better allies." Discussion topics have included how to be an **ally**, the "T" in **LGBTQ**, the language of diversity, and a video series focused on people with disabilities. More organizations, in both the public and private sectors, recognize that inclusion is a key ingredient to achieving organizational goals. If they truly want their employees to bring their whole selves to work—if they want to create environments of psychological safety, where differences are appreciated and understood, inclusive conversations are critical.

SUMMARY

> Learning to engage in inclusive conversations is critical for organizations that want to foster diversity, equity, and belonging.

> Inclusive conversations are needed in the workplace, in our educational institutions, and with children, about religion, politics, and other aspects of society where vast inequities exist.

> The stakes are higher than they have ever been to learn to engage in inclusive conversations given the global sociopolitical climate marked by polarization and intolerance.

> Employees are encouraged to bring their whole selves to work and bring multiple aspects of their identities that may be impacted by the socioeconomic climate.

> Employees are more vocal about sociopolitical events, and many expect their organizations to take a stand on issues.

> We need to teach children how to engage in inclusive conversations as they are very impacted by the current climate, and they notice differences in race, gender, and other aspects of identity at an early age.

Discussion/Reflection Questions

1. What is the rationale in your organization for learning how to engage in inclusive conversations?

2. To what extent do you have effective conversations across different dimensions of diversity? What makes them effective? Ineffective? What would make them more effective?

3. To what extent do you personally feel comfortable talking about diversity topics? Which ones are you most/least comfortable with? Why?

4. What are the personal/organizational benefits of learning how to have inclusive conversations?

5. Why is it important to have inclusive conversations with children?

-{ TWO }-

Conditions for Inclusive Conversations

Inclusive conversations require the right conditions. You have to know something about human diversity dimensions and the historical, sociological, and psychological factors that have dictated how we engage with each other. It is imperative to acknowledge and understand the systemic barriers to inclusion, equity, and belonging.

Too many of us minimize the challenges in engaging in inclusive conversations. We think that all that is required is positive intent and a genuine desire for equity. It takes much more than good intentions, however. A number of conditions are required for inclusive conversations. These eight important conditions are (1) commitment; (2) cultural competence; (3) brave and psychologically safe spaces; (4) understanding equity and **power**; (5) the ability to address fear and fragility; (6) **grace** and **forgiveness**; (7) **trust** and empathy; and (8) belonging and inclusion. This chapter briefly summarizes these conditions.

Condition 1: Commitment

I have been a diversity, equity, and inclusion (DEI) practitioner for more than 35 years, and I contend that we have not fundamentally changed the structures and systems that either maintain or worsen the conditions for historically **subordinated groups**. I often tell my audiences that I could have been standing before them in 1985 with the same message, discussing the same issues of inequitable systems that disadvantage certain groups.[1] Not nearly enough has changed in thirty-five years. It will take commitment and collective responsibility to change the trajectory.

The dictionary defines "commitment" as a state of being dedicated to a cause or activity. Many of us dedicate ourselves to causes that relate to things we are interested in such as climate change or a hobby such as golf. Think about something that you are dedicated to and the time and effort that you put into it to achieve your goal in that activity. If you are really dedicated, I dare say that it is quite a bit of time and effort. What is your real level of commitment to DEI? Are you involved because it is a part of your job? Does your interest stem from being personally impacted by DEI-related issues? For example, were you denied an opportunity because of your race, gender, gender identity, disability, or other dimension of difference? Are you dedicated because someone close to you experienced an inequity? Are you committed because you understand that it will take many voices and collective responsibility for change to happen on a large scale?

"Collective responsibility," which has also been referred to as "collective guilt," is the social justice concept that individuals are responsible for other people's actions by tolerating, ignoring, or harboring them, without actively collaborating in these actions.[2] In other words, even if you did not or do not personally participate in perpetuating injustices, we are all responsible for stopping them. Dr. Martin Luther King Jr. said it this way: "I can never be what I ought to be until you are what you ought to be, and you can never be what you ought to be until I am what I ought to be. This is the inter-related structure of reality."[3]

Collective action means that we are not complicit by being silent. If we say nothing or do nothing when we are aware of and or witness obvious injustices, we are complicit and are guilty of condoning the injustice. Dr. Martin Luther King Jr. also said: "The ultimate tragedy is not the oppression and cruelty by the bad people but the silence over that by the good people."[4] More recently, in the Netflix documentary *Hello, Privilege. It's Me, Chelsea*, the comedian Chelsea Handler speaks about how white privilege shows up in American culture. She sums up commitment this way: "It's about advocating in all spaces even times when it makes you uncomfortable—a lifelong, daily, 100% being committed to showing up for racial justice for the rest of your life."[5]

Inclusive conversations are for naught if the parties are not committed to taking action for change. Inclusive conversations to foster cross-cultural understanding are a start but need to be followed with ongoing, consistent action to ameliorate inequities.

Condition 2: Cultural Competence

As I stressed in my book *We Can't Talk about That at Work*, specific skills and abilities are required for inclusive conversations. "Cultural competence" can be defined as a continuous learning process to gain knowledge, skills, and understanding to discern cultural difference in one's own and other cultures and to use in problem solving, decision-making, and conflict resolution. Key skills to engage in inclusive conversations include gaining more cultural understanding of oneself and others, learning to listen to one's own assumptions and stereotypes, intentionally working to mitigate unconscious and conscious bias, choosing curiosity over judgment, and pausing and reflecting often. Chapter 3 explores self-understanding and specific skills to enhance the capability to effectively engage in inclusive conversations.

Condition 3: Brave and Psychologically Safe Spaces

Inclusive conversations push the boundaries of comfortable, safe spaces to brave spaces. Brave spaces create an environment that makes previously uncomfortable conversations safe to explore. The goal is first to create brave spaces to create **psychological safety.** Brave and psychological safe spaces are created in a culture where differences are acknowledged, understood, leveraged, and valued. Chapter 4 explores these conditions.

Condition 4: Understanding Equity and Power

Equity is the most important condition for inclusive conversations. Equity is different from equality. Equality means treating everyone the same. Equity is the treatment of people according to what they need and deserve, with an underlying assumption that some groups have historically been denied what they need due to entrenched inequitable systems. Equity means everyone has access to the resources, opportunities, and power they need to reach their full potential. Systems of power often thwart efforts to create equity. Inclusive conversations consider power dynamics. Chapter 5 examines equity and power.

Condition 5: The Ability to Address Fear and Fragility

Many people are afraid of talking about diversity and inclusion topics for fear they might get it wrong and will not be forgiven. Acknowledging and understanding these fears is an all-important step in engaging in inclusive conversations. Fear and fragility are related. Fear can induce fragility and by the same token fragility can lead to fear. Chapter 6 provides advice on how to have inclusive conversations in the midst of fear and fragility.

Condition 6: Grace and Forgiveness

Unless we are willing to forgive at the individual, interpersonal, and systems level for wrongs that we have endured, inclusive conversations will get little traction. Spiritual leaders and behavioral scientists remind us that forgiveness is more for the victim than the perpetrator. Forgiveness does not mean that we forget the transgression. Grace is related to forgiveness. It is unearned consideration. Grace and forgiveness recognize that none of us is perfect and that we are all learning. Chapter 7 delves into this condition.

Condition 7: Trust and Empathy

Trust and empathy are necessary conditions for inclusive conversations. Building trust across different dimensions of diversity is complex. A history of inhumane treatment contributes to the lack of trust. Even though some of this treatment is no longer legal, multigenerational memory and damage impedes the ability to create trusting cross-cultural relationships. Empathy fosters trust, and trust engenders empathy. Chapter 8 explores trust and empathy.

Condition 8: Belonging and Inclusion

Belonging and inclusion go hand in hand. Inclusion is the intersection of a sense of belonging and where a person feels appreciated for their uniqueness. Chapter 9 explores these conditions for inclusion conversations.

Inclusive Conversations Are Not Easy

We must create conditions that allow us to have deep, meaningful conversations across difference. Even when all of the conditions are in place for inclusive conversations, they are not easy. Discussing race, ethnicity, gender, gender identity, and other dimensions of diversity make many of us very uncomfortable. It takes intentionality, commitment, and persistence.

SUMMARY

> Inclusive conversations are not easy and require a number of conditions to make them successful.

> Historical injustices make inclusive conversations especially difficult. We have to consider the psychological and sociological implications for engaging in inclusive conversations.

> Accepting personal and collective responsibility for correcting societal injustices is a critical condition for inclusive conversations.

Discussion/Reflection Questions

1. Which conditions exist in your organization for inclusive conversations? Which conditions are not present? Why?

2. What is your reason for being personally committed to engage in inclusive conversations? What is the organizational reason? How does the commitment show up on a day-to-day basis?

3. To what extent are you/your organization knowledgeable of the historical, psychological, and sociological implications for engaging in inclusive conversations?

4. What do you/your organization do to enhance your knowledge of the historical, psychological, and sociological implications for engaging in inclusive conversations?

⊣ THREE ⊢

First Learn How
to Talk to Yourself

> Spend time in intentional self-reflection to enhance self-understanding and gain clarity on your values, beliefs, assumptions, biases, and judgments.

The ability to engage in inclusive conversations is a skill to be developed and honed. It is a necessary ingredient for cultural competence—a continuous learning process to gain knowledge and understanding of your own and other cultures, to be able to discern cultural patterns for more effective problem solving, decision-making, and conflict resolution. The journey to developing cultural competence includes three key skills that start with self-understanding after which you should focus on understanding your cultural "others." Once you develop those two skills, you are ready to have inclusive conversations to effectively bridge across differences. Inclusive conversations require an advanced skill set and can happen only when the first two skills have been developed.

Talking to Yourself Fosters Self-Understanding

Self-understanding is essential to being able to dialogue across different dimensions of diversity. Understanding why you believe what you believe, where those beliefs come from, what has formed your worldview and created your particular mind-set is critical for effective inclusive conversations. The ability to critically reflect on interactions you have with others in your circle, those outside of your circle, and even strangers can help you to better understand your core beliefs and prepare for inclusive conversations. One of the best ways to better understand yourself is to spend time literally talking to yourself.

There is somewhat of a stigma associated with "talking to yourself." Others may judge or criticize this practice. We may laugh and think that someone has a loose screw if we witness them talking to themselves out loud. However, we talk to ourselves all of the time, whether we realize it or not. You ask yourself questions about mundane day-to-day decisions as well as more important potentially life-altering decisions. Thinking is actually a form of talking to yourself. According to clinical psychologist Dr. Jessica Nicolosi, talking to ourselves out loud forces us to slow down our thoughts and process them differently because we engage the language centers of our brain. She says that when we talk to ourselves, we become more deliberate, which creates a slower process to think, feel, and act. In the same way we look to trusted companions for advice, Nicolosi says that we can talk to ourselves. This occurs when we're experiencing a deep emotion, such as anger, fear, or other stressors. She says that it is typically some emotion that **triggers** us to speak out loud.[1] Engaging in inclusive conversations can be stressful and triggering, and therefore self-talk is really important.

Intentionally spending time talking to yourself on a regular basis—both in quiet, thoughtful contemplation and out loud dissecting your daily thoughts, feelings, and actions—fosters self-understanding. Make it a new habit. Take self-talk to another level by keeping a journal and writing down your perspectives on your cross-cultural experiences and your interpretation of situations that you might hear or see in the media. In other words, have an inclusive conversation with yourself.

If you really listened to yourself, what are you thinking, what are you saying to yourself that you would not say out loud? What are you saying out loud that you really don't believe but feel societal pressure to respond in a socially acceptable way? What drives your thoughts? How are your thoughts connected to your behaviors? What biases do you know that you have? All of these self-talk questions are key to self-understanding and enhance your ability to engage in inclusive conversations.

Focus on Self Is Not to Be Confused with Egocentrism or Individualism

The type of self-focus that I advocate should not be equated with egocentrism, a worldview that considers only one's own cultural perspective and the inability to consider the perspective of other cultures.[2] The self-reflection that is important for inclusive conversations is in service of learning how to more effectively engage with others. I am simply saying that the prerequisite for effectively engaging with others is deep self-knowledge and self-reflection.

Individualism is a value that has historically been associated with Western culture. It is defined as being motivated by personal rewards and benefits. The "I" is bigger than the "we." In **individualistic cultures**, goals are established based on individual wants and desires. People see themselves as independent beings free to operate on their own. This worldview is contrasted to **collectivist cultures**, more associated with Eastern parts of the world, which prioritize the group or society over individuals. In these cultures, people view themselves as interdependent and are taught to do what is best for society as a whole rather than themselves as individuals. Based on their origins from collectivist cultures, **African Americans, Asian Americans, Latinx,** and **Native Americans** tend to be more collectivist than individualistic in the United States. For example, people with a collectivist mind-set might find exercises that focus on self more difficult because they cannot separate self from their connection to the larger society. By the same token, extreme individualism may impede our ability to see our connection to others and our **collective responsibility** for engaging at a societal level.

I posit that it is "both/and"—that is, we have to be able to see ourselves as individuals and also importantly as a part of the larger society comprised of systems that define our reality. The US individualistic idiom is "Pull yourself up by your own bootstraps." This should be tempered with a more collectivist view that also considers those who have no boots and therefore perhaps need help from others. The idea of collective responsibility discussed in Chapter 2 may be an easier notion to digest for collectivist cultures.

Some sociologists argue that even as individuals our worldviews are shaped by our environments, experiences, and power structures. So there is really no independent or truly individualistic thinking, or as the saying goes, "There is no such thing as a view from nowhere." The understanding of self is inextricably tied to our interpretations of history, power, politics, and other factors.

Sociologist Stuart Hall says that the work of understanding self and identity is more about "deconstructing" than "discovery."[3]

Learning to Practice Metacognition

Metacognition is an approach for deconstructing. It is the ability to think about and regulate one's own thoughts. It is thinking about thinking and the ability through the process of thinking about thinking to change your thoughts.[4] This concept is gaining popularity in how teachers train students to approach a task. It has been described as "knowing about knowing," becoming "aware of one's awareness" and the ability to engage in higher-order thinking skills. Metacognition refers to a level of thinking that involves active control over the process of thinking that is used in learning situations.

There are three stages of metacognitive thinking as it relates to inclusive conversations: planning, monitoring, and evaluation. During the planning phase, ask yourself:

> What will be required to engage in this inclusive conversation?

> Have I done anything like this in the past?

> What do I already know about the topic of this conversation (e.g., race, sexual orientation, gender dynamics, and other dimensions of difference)?

> What do I want as the outcome of this conversation?

> Is this a debate or a dialogue? Am I trying to win an argument or learn something new?

During the monitoring stage, which happens during the conversation, the key self-reflective questions include:

> Is the conversation leading toward the original goal?

> How well am I doing in practicing inclusion in this conversation? Am I keeping an open mind, or am I starting to be judgmental? Am I really listening to understand? Should I be asking more clarifying questions? Are we still dialoguing, or are we moving toward debate? Are there things being said that are triggering for me? Why?

The third stage of metacognitive thinking is evaluation, after the conversation. Ask yourself:

> How did I do? Did I achieve the goal?

> What could I have done differently?

> What biases did I notice surfacing in my thinking?

> What do I need to learn for these types of conversations to go better the next time?

> What made me say? How would I interpret the other person's response? What in my life's experiences made that a trigger for me? Why did I interpret that situation so differently from the other person?

Some experts in metacognition have expanded the idea and embrace social metacognition, which includes the influence of culture and our self-concept on how we think.[5]

Self-Talk Helps Us to Manage Our Unconscious Bias

Unconscious bias is a very popular topic in the diversity, equity, and inclusion (DEI) arena today. I am often asked, "If my biases are unconscious, how do I know that I have them?" If we engage in metacognition, it is easier for us to bring what is unconscious to our consciousness. Our unconscious biases usually trigger a behavior or a thought that we verbalize. For example, "We always recruit from these schools because we get good talent." Asking yourself why you said that and why you might be biased toward those schools can help you to be open to other options. Consider the statement: "I am okay with hiring underrepresented groups as long as they are qualified." Asking yourself why you think an underrepresented group would not be qualified is metacognitive thinking. Learning to think metacognitively is a skill and habit that will enhance your capability for inclusive conversations.

The Role of Self-Concept in Effective Inclusive Conversations

Self-concept is influenced by social identities. A person's social identity is their sense of who they are based on their group membership. Social psychologist Henri Tajfel proposed that the groups to which we belong (e.g., social class, family, race, ethnicity, nationality, profession, etc.) are an important source of pride and **self-esteem**.[6] Research shows that people are motivated to have a positive social identity. When we feel connected to a social group (called **social group identity**), our self-esteem is higher and we feel safe and accepted.[7] In contrast, when people feel excluded, rejected, or ignored by others, they experience hurt and pain and are likely to withdraw from the interaction.[8]

All of us belong to more than one social identity group, known as **intersectionality**. More and more employees are invited to bring their "whole" selves to work. The idea of "whole self" acknowledges that we have multiple identities that intersect and overlap. The term "intersectionality" was coined by Kimberle

FIGURE 3.1 Fostering Self-Understanding
Source: Property of The Winters Group, Inc.

Crenshaw, professor at Columbia Law School and the University of California Los Angeles, to address the perpetual exclusion of Black women in feminist, antiracist discourse. Intersectionality recognizes that group identities (e.g. race, gender, sexuality, class, age) overlap and intersect in dynamic ways that shape an individual's experience.[9] Ask yourself, who am I and how do my multiple identities influence how I think about myself and others? The Winters Group uses an exercise that invites individuals to think about their intersecting identities (Figure 3.1). In which identities do you find yourself as a part of the **dominant group** or the **subordinated group**?

Dominant group membership might naturally lead to a more positive self-image, whereas membership in a subordinated group might engender feelings of inadequacy. Dominant groups are those with **systemic power**, privileges, and social status within a society. Conversely, subordinated groups are those that have been traditionally and historically oppressed, excluded, or disadvantaged in society. The concept of dominant and subordinated groups is explored more in Chapter 5.

Your position of dominance or subordination can influence your self-concept. Is your self-concept always positive? Do you have doubts about your capabilities that might play out as imposter syndrome or internalized oppression? **Imposter syndrome** is defined as feelings of inadequacy or incompetence despite demonstrated evidence of success.[10] Behavorial scientists have found that women are more likely to experience the imposter syndrome than men.

Internalized oppression is a phenomenon usually associated with historically **marginalized** groups, where we begin to believe the negative stereotypes that are perpetuated by society. Self-reflecting on the extent to which these negative self-concepts are impeding your ability to engage fully and authentically in an inclusive conversation is key. Why do I feel inferior in this situation? What am I thinking about myself? How is it manifesting in my tone, my demeanor, my words? There may be a great deal of internal conflict as marginalized groups try to find their place in systems that unwittingly perpetuate inequities. Questions like "Is there something wrong with me?" might surface regularly.

This is why employee affinity groups are important in larger organizations to provide space for discussing common concerns. For those in dominant groups, questions might be different, such as "Am I even relevant anymore? It seems like everything is about gays or Blacks. What about the ordinary white man?" These concerns need to be addressed by individuals before engaging in inclusive conversations. For example, a white male might ask himself, "What evidence do I have that 'everything' is about gays and Blacks? Why is that my perception?" Practicing metacognitive thinking can support such self-inquiry and foster greater self-understanding.

Negative self-talk can impede progress in inclusive conversations. Focusing on a positive self-image is critical. Remind yourself of your accomplishments and your inherent worth. Try to tune out thoughts of inferiority or inadequacy and replace them with positive thoughts about who you are. Those from historically marginalized groups might ask themselves questions like these:

> Have you internalized the stereotype of angry Black woman or threatening Black man?

> Is your self-concept limited by your physical abilities? Have you internalized negative self-talk that you are just somebody in a wheelchair who others pity?

> Do you talk about yourself in negative ways because English is not your first language and to many you speak with an accent? Do you think that they think you are not as smart?

> Do you think about yourself as irrelevant because you are a baby boomer still in the workplace and you feel out of touch with so many younger people taking leadership roles?

Developing a positive self-concept is a journey that starts early in one's life. I recently saw a news clip of a three-year-old African American boy on his way to preschool. His parents had taught him to constantly remind himself "you are smart, you are blessed, and you can do anything." The clip showed the boy chanting this over and over with a big smile on his face as he made his way to his first day of school. What is your positive self-talk chant?

Understand Your Styles and Your Preferences

There are many psychological tools and concepts that can support you in better understanding yourself and how you might approach inclusive conversations. The Myers–Briggs Type Indicator supports your understanding of your personality type. Are you extroverted or introverted? Judging or perceiving? An introvert might need more time to process, whereas an extrovert might process out loud in an inclusive conversation and be annoyed that the introvert is not doing the same. Emergenetics is a tool that is rooted in the concept that who you are today is the emergence of your behavior, genetic makeup, and life experiences.[11] The Emergenetics Profile assesses you on four "Thinking Attributes" (conceptual, structural, social, and analytical) and three "Behavioral Attributes" (flexibility, assertiveness, and expressiveness). The extent to which we are skilled in emotional intelligence traits (emotional self-awareness, emotional self-management, awareness of the emotions of others feelings, and ability to effectively manage group emotions) influences the extent to which we can have effective cross-difference conversations.[12] Emotional intelligence is well recognized today as a necessary skill for good leadership.

Another very useful self-awareness tool is the **Intercultural Development Inventory**, which measures our capability to effectively bridge across diversity dimensions.[13] The theory says that either we see the world only from our own cultural frame, or we have a mind-set that allows us to understand the complexities of culture—a multicultural worldview—recognizing patterns in our own and other cultures to achieve mutually respectful outcomes. Most people who take the tool fall at **minimization** on the scale. Minimization is a place on the Intercultural Development

Continuum where similarities are emphasized and prioritized and therefore differences might be missed. For example, someone at minimization might proudly declare that they are color-blind. They might say "people are just people and any differences really don't matter." I explain why this is problematic in the case scenario below, "I Don't See Race."

The Intercultural Conflict Style Inventory (ICS) is another tool to help us understand how we prefer to respond to conflict based on our culturally learned behaviors.[14] Do you prefer to be direct or indirect in your communication? Emotionally expressive or controlled? Being aware of your conflict style and how it differs from another's is an important consideration when engaging in inclusive conversations. The results of these types of tools can help in your self-understanding as well as understanding others. It is critical for inclusive conversations to understand your natural ways of being. For example, if your Emergenetics Profile reveals that you are a very conceptual person (big picture, visionary, imaginative, learns by experimenting) and you're attempting a conversation with someone who is very structural (logical, likes guidelines, cautious of new ideas, learns by doing), it may take some adapting to each other's styles before you are able to have a meaningful conversation.

CASE SCENARIO
(Emergenetics Styles)
Was It My Age?

You are a baby boomer leader. One of your millennial employees comes to you with what she thinks is a great idea. She shares the general concept with you. Your style is structural, while the millennial's style is conceptual. You display confusion and give her feedback that you cannot envision how this idea can possibility be implemented in your organization. It is too far afield from anything that has ever been done. You tell her that in the future, before she brings such an idea, it would be helpful if she thinks it through more and considers the steps for implementation. The millennial leaves frustrated because she had hoped for a brainstorming session where the two of you would "imagine" the viability of the concept. She feels shut down and thinks that you are not taking her seriously because she is younger and newer to the organization.

The conversation might have gone better if both were aware of their different styles, acknowledged them upfront, and agreed on how the meeting should go to adapt to each of their preferences. The leader could have been more open and asked questions like, "Tell me a little more about the details?" The millennial employee might have been prepared to flesh out more of the details to account for her leader's structural style.

CASE SCENARIO
(Intercultural Development Continuum)
"I Don't See Race"

Consider two co-workers engaged in conversation, one white and the other Black. The white employee says to the Black employee, "I don't really see your color. Your race makes no difference." This sounds very much like a minimization statement. An inclusive conversation might sound something like this:

BLACK EMPLOYEE: While I understand that your intent is positive, the impact of such a statement is hurtful because it makes me feel that you are saying that you do not see me. It minimizes my racial identity, which is very important to me, and I want you to acknowledge it so that we can better discuss both our differences and similarities.

WHITE EMPLOYEE: Wow, it was not my intent to demean you. I thought it was a positive comment, and I would like to understand more about you and your perspectives.

This kind of conversation will be much more successful if they each have had some education on identities and perhaps have taken the Intercultural Development Inventory. Without having worked through some self-understanding, this could not have been an inclusive conversation.

At the conclusion of this conversation, the white employee should engage in some metacognitive self-talk, which might include questions like this:

> What do I need to learn for these types of conversations to go better the next time?

> What made me say that to my co-worker? How do I interpret my co-worker's response?

> Am I open to change?

Self-understanding is a lifelong endeavor and one that many of us neglect. We cannot learn and grow if we do not engage in ongoing, intentional self-talk and self-reflection to understand who and why we are. Self-understanding means critically examining our thoughts, feelings, and behaviors and the cultural influences that have shaped them.

SUMMARY

> Talk to yourself out loud to slow down your thinking, feeling, and acting.

> Practice metacognition. Think about what you are thinking to manage your biases.

> Know where you have power and use it to advance inclusion.

> Cultivate a positive self-concept and embrace your multiple intersecting identities.

> Learn about your natural styles, preferences, and worldviews as well as those of others.

> Acknowledge different personalities, styles, preferences, and competencies at the beginning of conversations to honor your differences and increase the likelihood of achieving the goals of the inclusive conversation.

Discussion/Reflection Questions

1. How much time do you spend in self-exploration, asking yourself why you believe what you believe, why you think what you think?

2. To what extent do you understand how your intersecting identities influence your worldview?

3. How much time do you spend considering how and why others might have a different worldview? How open are you to listening, understanding, and accepting other (even opposing) opinions?

4. What assessments have you taken that help you understand who you are? What assessments has your work team taken, and how do you use the information to engage in inclusive conversations?

5. How much time do you spend as a group discussing your similarities and differences and how they influence your team interactions? What can you do to enhance your understanding of your similarities and differences?

FOUR

Creating Brave, Psychologically Safe Spaces

> What if we first created brave spaces so that more people could feel safe speaking their truths?

In the introduction I shared an example of a situation where a leader asked me how he might have been brave in the moment. In a meeting where participants were encouraged to share their personal diversity, equity, and inclusion (DEI) journeys, he shared a time when he upset an LGBTQ employee by mistakenly using the wrong terminology to refer to them (the employee's preferred pronoun). His purpose for sharing this situation was to illustrate that we will make mistakes and can recover from them if we are willing to acknowledge and learn from them. As he was sharing the story, several in the audience of about three hundred snickered and laughed. Although this leader was not sure what sparked laughter, it made him feel very uncomfortable. He thought perhaps the laughter was targeted at the particular reference to LGBTQ community.

While the appropriate approach depends on a number of variables, if the condition of brave, psychologically safe space exists in the organization, I advised him to share how the laughter made him feel using an "I" statement. He might say something like: "While I don't know what promoted the laughter, and in the spirit of bravery, I want to share the impact. It made me feel uncomfortable because I was sharing a serious, deeply personal example of how to recover from mistakes. I am concerned how the laughter might be interpreted by others. I want to be sure we are fostering inclusion and belonging and to be able to continue to have open conversations on difficult topics."

This approach comes with risks. In a perfect world of brave spaces, the risks are lower. However, in the imperfect world that most of us exist in, we have to consider the risks and other conditions for inclusive conversations such as the power dynamics discussed in Chapter 5. In this scenario the person sharing the story is a leader and therefore his position afforded him the positional power to call out the behavior. If you are not in a position of power, in a brave space organization, we would hope that someone in power would call out the behavior. If that does not happen, it may be safer to share the impact with your manager, mentor, or human resources representative expecting that they would take action to communicate the impact to all in attendance.

From Safety to Bravery

Inclusive conversations push the boundaries of safety to bravery. Creating brave zones is a condition that allows for the surfacing and sharing of each other's deep truths without fear of retribution. It is a space where it is expected that there may be discomfort, where you might feel some anxiety, ambiguity, and even discord as opposing perspectives are shared. It is also a space where you feel safe enough to be brave, to push the boundaries of **political correctness** and obligatory, unchallenging small talk.

Safety often means something different for dominant groups than it does for subordinated groups in inclusive conversations. For dominant groups, when discussing race in particular, "safety" more often means that "you will not make me feel uncomfortable." For groups that have been historically marginalized, "safety" often means that "I can make you feel uncomfortable (even if that is not necessarily my intention) and you will listen without defensiveness, dismissiveness, and **whitesplaining**" (a concept defined in Chapter 10).

Dominant groups in an organizational and societal context set the rules and therefore rarely move beyond safety as defined by those groups. For subordinated groups, experience has taught them that if you name the reality of your experiences of **oppression**, exclusion, and a sense of not belonging, you risk being labeled as overly sensitive or misguided. Conversation either shuts down completely or it reverts to less meaningful "safe" topics. Relationships may be damaged or completely ruined. In either case, inclusive conversations are no longer possible nor is the condition of psychological safety.

Psychological Safety

"Psychological safety" is defined as the belief that you will not be punished if you make a mistake.[1] Psychological safety describes individuals' perceptions about the consequences of interpersonal risks in their environment.[2] People who are psychologically safe feel free to speak up about problems and sensitive issues. One's perception of psychological safety is based on a belief about the group norm. If the norm in the culture is that we can talk about uncomfortable topics, that we are open to hearing opposing views, the condition of psychological safety is likely present.

How do you know if your environment is psychologically safe? Some of the ways to assess psychological safety are offered by researcher A. Edmondson in the article "Psychological Safety and Learning Behavior in Work Teams."[3] Are the following conditions present in your organization or workplace?

> When someone makes a mistake, it is often held against them.

> In this team it is easy to discuss difficult issues and problems.

> In this team people are sometimes rejected for being different.

> It is completely safe to take a risk on this team.

> It is difficult to ask other members of this team for help.

> Members of this team value and respect each other's contributions.

Creating Brave Spaces First

The typical narrative is that people have to first feel safe before they can be brave. But what if the order was the opposite? What if we create spaces where people can be brave so that we can all eventually feel safe? I am not suggesting that people, particularly those from historically marginalized groups, have to risk being misunderstood, ridiculed, or otherwise outed for people to feel safe. However, I am suggesting that until we address the roots of psychological danger (the opposite of psychological safety)—exclusive mind-sets and policies—by creating spaces in which everyone is encouraged to delve into their own discomfort and learn about who they are, who others are, and how we can be bridges for one another, we will not be able to create sustainably safe places.

If we use that definition of bravery, it could be considered brave to ask questions of yourself—about your identity, your culture, your biases, as outlined in Chapter 3. It could be brave to explore how you relate to your cultural "others" and how you are able, or unable, to bridge gaps in cultural understanding. It could be brave to simply have conversations with those whose views are different from yours and to be inclusive of those views (unless those ideas are harmful to you or anyone else). It could be brave to delve into some of the ways in which you have been marginalized (or have marginalized others) and to see those instances against the backdrop of inequitable systems.

If this is bravery, then bravery leads to safety. Once you've been able to share deeply about who you are and what you believe in, even with those you'd never thought you would agree with, perhaps you'll see that the possibilities for human connection go beyond what you could have imagined in this polarized world. In the end, the conversation about safe spaces should not be a battle between those who feel safe and those who don't. Rather, it should be a conversation about how we can all benefit from being brave enough to be who we are and see the person across from us in all of who they want to be. Ultimately, we will all feel safer when we are no longer strangers to ourselves and to each other.

Are We Ready for Psychologically Safe and Brave Conversations?

Many of our environments are just not ready for brave conversations about race, ethnicity, religion, gender, and other dimensions of difference, and to push it too soon is to regress from any progress made. As I discussed at length in *We Can't Talk about That at Work*, getting to inclusive conversations is a developmental process that requires meeting people where they are. Those of us who are activists and practitioners in the DEI space can get very frustrated with our colleagues who don't want to have the tough conversations. I contend that for many they just don't know how and will retreat into a noncommunicative, unhealthy place—obviously not the desired outcome. We cannot just will brave spaces because we want them.

If we jump right into brave spaces without the conditions discussed in Chapter 2, we run the risk of disrupting long-held beliefs in ways that shock the system. Often the conversation space is limited to a two- to four-hour onetime session limiting the opportunity to develop trust and brave spaces. Both dominant and subordinated groups might leave such sessions feeling traumatized. That trauma may play out as shock and denial as described in Chapter 6 for dominant groups, and for subordinated groups it may just deepen and/or open already painful wounds. Inclusive conversation sessions have to be structured in ways that acknowledge the pain and offer some type of follow-up to address the potential trauma.

The book *The Art of Effective Facilitation* has a chapter called "From Safe Spaces to Brave Spaces: A New Way to Frame Dialogue around Diversity and Social Justice."[4] The authors share an experience with a group of college students training to be resident assistants in college dorms. They facilitated a popular experiential exercise designed to help participants understand **privilege**, a concept defined in Chapter 5. The exercise calls for the group to form a line. The facilitator then shares a series of statements and if the statement pertains to you, you step forward, if not you step back. Some sample statements include:

> ➤ If your ancestors were forced to come to the United States not by choice, take one step back.

> ➤ If your primary ethnic identity is "American," take one step forward.

> ➤ If you were ever called names because of your race, class, ethnicity, gender, or sexual orientation, take one step back.

> ➤ If there were people who worked for your family as servants, gardeners, nannies, and so on, take one step forward.

> ➤ If you were ever ashamed or embarrassed by your clothes, house, car, and so on, take one step back.

> ➤ If one or both of your parents were "white collar" professionals (doctors, lawyers, etc.), take one step forward.

Usually participants who hold dominant group identities finish the exercise in the front of the room, and those of subordinated group identities in the back. To the facilitators' surprise and dismay, the exercise did not go well. Students who held dominant group identities felt "persecuted, blamed and negatively judged."

You are entering a brave zone where we have Bold, Inclusive Conversations...

In this space...
> We face our fears and name them.
> We choose curiosity over judgment.
> We consider the impact, not just the intent, behind our words and actions.
> We lean into discomfort, recognizing it as a space of growth.
> We admit when we are being fragile.
> We welcome others to point out our fragility when needed.
> We acknowledge our collective imperfections so that we can make mistakes.
> We forgive often.
> We call people "in" rather than call people "out."
> We seek authenticity.
> We embody our truths.

FIGURE 4.1 Conditions for a Brave Zone
Source: The Winters Group, Inc.

Subordinated students said the exercise was a painful reminder of their daily lived experiences. They also said that it put them in the role of teaching their dominant group colleagues about their different experiences, which is exhausting. This is a prime example of lack of readiness to have inclusive conversations. Without having first conducted foundational education to build skills in self-understanding and understanding others, these types of exercises can do more harm than good and shut down meaningful dialogue.

In Figure 4.1, The Winters Group has developed some conditions that are designed to create brave spaces for inclusive conversations. However, we use them only with advanced groups who have some competency in diversity, equity, and inclusion concepts and who we feel are ready to embrace them. I discuss fear, fragility, and forgiveness as well as calling people in rather than out in later chapters.

Who Doesn't Enjoy Psychological Safety to Speak Up?

These days employees are encouraged to bring their whole selves to work. Leaders have learned that employees will be more productive and engaged to the extent that they feel that they can be authentic, openly sharing their feelings and nonwork-related aspects of who they are. Although this might sound like a great way to foster psychological safety and brave spaces for dialogue, for those in subordinated groups this is often a joke. I have heard many people of color laugh and say, "Are you kidding me? They could not handle my whole self. I can bring only the self that is most like the dominant group." People with nonvisible disabilities may not want to share that aspect of their identity, fearing that it could limit their career opportunities. In the 2016 *Fortune* article, "An Inside Look at What's Keeping Black Men out of the Executive Suite," research shows that Black men report that they have to constantly **code-shift** (explained in Chapter 9), needing to appear "focused in the office but not too aggressive, hungry but not too threating, well-dressed but not showy, talented but not too talented."[5] The energy expended not bringing your full self to work can be exhausting.

In a study conducted by David Hekman and colleagues, published in the journal of the *Academy of Management* in 2016, they found clear and consistent evidence that women and people of color who promote diversity are penalized in terms of how others perceive their competence and effectiveness.[6] The researchers interviewed 350 executives on several diversity-valuing behaviors—for example, whether they respected cultural, religious, gender, and racial differences; valued working with a diverse group of people; and felt comfortable managing people from different racial or cultural backgrounds. They defined "diversity-valuing behavior" as that which promotes demographic balance within organizations. Their conclusion was that when white men vocally valued diversity, they were not rated less competent, but women and people of color who advocated for diversity were. Women and people of color are more apt to come under attack when they speak out for those in their identity group, in a way that white men are not.[7]

A study by the National Bureau of Economic research showed that Black people have to perform better than their white counterparts.[8] The study found that Black workers are more closely scrutinized, which increases the chances of errors being caught, and the result is that Black workers were more likely to be let go for "errors," thereby making it less safe to make a mistake. Many LGBTQ employees still do not feel safe bringing their whole selves to work. According to research by the Human Rights Campaign Foundation, 46 percent of LGBTQ employees are not open about their sexuality at work for fear of being stereotyped, making people feel uncomfortable, or losing connections with co-workers—a statistic that has not changed much since 2008.[9]

Women are more often labeled as having an "aggressive" communication style. A 2019 study reported in the *Harvard Business Review* looked at two hundred performance reviews from one company. The study counted the number of references to being "too aggressive" in the reviews and found that 76 percent of the instances of aggressiveness were attributed to women, while only 24 percent of men were identified as having such a communication style.[10] This type of feedback leads to women questioning themselves and perhaps not speaking up as much. Those in dominant groups may not feel safe to discuss issues faced by historically subordinated groups. As was the case with the students mentioned above who experienced the privilege walk exercise, they may feel guilt, judgment, and apprehension, which might shut down inclusive conversations.

While organizations have good intentions when they declare their desire for employees to bring their whole selves to work and to create psychologically safe environments, it is not easy and currently not a reality for many historically subordinated groups. It is just too risky to be yourself or to speak up about the inequities that you experience and witness. Dominant groups also stay silent fearing retribution for unintentionally saying something offensive.

Creating Brave and Psychologically Safe Spaces for Inclusive Conversations

Creating and sustaining psychologically safe spaces where inclusive conversations can occur in the workplace takes time, consistency, and intentionality. Here are some specific ways to foster and develop these conditions:

> **Develop group norms and create shared meaning.** What do we mean by "safe spaces" or "brave spaces"? What are specific examples (see Figure 4.1 for Brave Zone conditions)? What are the boundaries? Hold inclusive conversation sessions to brainstorm and gain clarity on these definitions. Start each conversation reminding the parties of the norms. Redefine

terms as needed. If these norms had existed in the example at the beginning of the chapter, calling out the laughter might have been easier for the organization leader.

> **Acknowledge that the extent to which safety and bravery are experienced varies by identity group.**

> **Learn about and discuss the historical, systemic inequities that continue to create unsafe environments for some groups.**

> **Listen to and validate the experiences of different identity groups.** If you are a leader, make sharing experiences a regular agenda item to build trust and thus encourage bravery. It may take time to break down barriers to get to safe and brave spaces. Be patient. Stick with it.

> **Pay more attention to and correct biases that perpetuate inequitable environments.** For example, if you are a leader with positional power, review each of your performance assessments. Do you use different language to describe the accomplishments of women versus men? People of color versus white employees? Why? Engage in self-reflection as recommended in Chapter 3 to better understand your biases. If you are a member of a historically subordinated group, question feedback that you don't understand or agree with. Ask for specific examples, like this: "Can you give me a specific instance where I was aggressive? In your mind, how might I have handled that situation in a less aggressive way?" If you don't agree, you might say something like: "I would like to offer a different interpretation of your example. I am a direct communicator and I was being professionally assertive. Can we talk more about the difference between

aggressive and assertiveness? I would like to continue to be effective and also authentic without being offensive or defensive. I don't want characterizations such as this to impede my progress."

> **Become an ally for subordinated groups.** A heterosexual, **cisgender** woman could be an ally for a LGBTQ colleague. The Anti-Oppression Network defines "allyship" as a lifelong process of building relationships based on trust, consistency, and accountability with marginalized individuals and groups of people.[11] It is not self-defined— our work must be recognized by the people we seek to ally ourselves with. Becoming a good ally is more than being interested in and passionate about equity, it requires really understanding how the inequities manifest for the group. A good ally will speak up and speak out for the subordinated identity in ways that are empathic and foster a sense of belonging.

Creating Psychologically Safe Spaces for Children

As pointed out earlier, according to a study by NPR's *Sesame Street* and the University of Chicago, parents do not talk with their children about human diversity issues. Another study indicated that children start to recognize racial differences as early as six months old. Today, with easy access to some of the harsh realities of the world through social media and other technological advances, it is not possible nor advisable to shield children. Bullying and suicide rates among young people are at an all-time high.[12] Children have to worry about their safety in school.

Current realities necessitate that we are intentional about having inclusive conversations with children.

Some specific actions you can take to create psychologically safe spaces for inclusive conversations with children include:

> **Be honest.** When children ask about something that may be difficult, don't minimize it. Broderick Sawyer, a clinical psychologist featured in Conscious Kid—an education, research, and policy organization dedicated to reducing bias and promoting positive identity development in youth— shared that the first thing you should ask a child who has faced discriminatory behavior is, "How did that make you feel?"[13] We must listen with encouragement and without judgment.

> **Consider vocabulary comprehension and experiences.** Use words that children will understand at their age level. If you are talking about sexual assault, rather than using an adult word like "assault," maybe "touching" is a better word coupled with showing the places where children should not be touched. Maybe you develop your own vocabulary for the parts of the body that are off-limits.

> **Connect new concepts to ideas or experiences they have encountered previously.** Make connections to situations that they will understand, such as "Remember the time when…"

> **Be sensitive to age-specific challenges.** Start conversations so that children can share in their own words what they are thinking or concerned about. Begin with: "Tell me, what are you thinking about?"

> **Leverage peer-created resources.** Find examples of young people talking or writing about diversity-related topics, maybe videos on YouTube that you can talk about.

> **Acknowledge different and even polarizing perspectives.** Start with something like: "You may hear people saying…" or "Some people believe…" and explain that "People care a lot about this and have many different ideas. Sometimes they might lead to arguments."

If we engage our children in inclusive conversations at an early age, it is more likely that they will be better equipped for effective dialogue about differences when they enter the workforce.

──────── SUMMARY ────────

> Safe spaces are achieved by first creating brave spaces for inclusive conversations.

> Brave spaces are not necessarily comfortable. They are designed to take us out of our comfort zones.

> Psychological safety is where people feel free to speak up about problems and even sensitive issues without retribution.

> Brave space dialogues may lead to identity-based trauma, which needs to be effectively addressed.

> Getting to brave spaces for inclusive conversations takes time and commitment.

> Research shows that women and people of color are more often penalized for speaking up for inclusion, suggesting that we may not feel safe to do so.

> Effective allyship is important in creating brave spaces for dialogue.

> It is important to create psychologically safe space for children to engage in age-appropriate inclusive conversations.

Discussion/Reflection Questions

1. How do you define safe spaces as contrasted to brave spaces? What is the difference?

2. To what extent is your environment safe for inclusive conversations? Brave? If it is not safe or brave, what needs to be done to create safe and brave spaces?

3. What happens in your environment when someone makes a mistake about diversity, equity, or inclusion issues?

4. How do you become a good ally, as defined in this chapter?

5. Why is it important to engage in brave conversations with children?

-{ FIVE }-

Seek Equity and Decenter Power

> Equity and power are inextricably entwined. Inclusive conversations must be equitable conversations and thus must consider power.

Equity is probably the most important condition for inclusive conversations. You really can't talk about equity without talking about power. "Equity" is defined as the treatment of people according to what they need and deserve. Equity means everyone has access to the resources, opportunities, and power they need to reach their full potential. In the context of diversity, equity, and inclusion (DEI), "power" is the ability to decide who has access to resources and the capacity to direct or influence the behavior of others, oneself, and/or the course of events. Power can be based on one's position or one's position, influence, and or privilege—defined as a system that maintains advantage and disadvantage based on social group memberships. Power thus operates, intentionally and unintentionally, on individual, institutional, and cultural levels.

The term "equity," while certainly not new in the lexicon, is fairly new in the corporate diversity and inclusion space. "Equity" is a more elusive and controversial term than "diversity" and "inclusion." There is still not a single definition for "diversity" and "inclusion" either, but equity seems to carry more contention than the other two. Perhaps we can think of diversity as the mix of differences in any particular setting to include (but not necessarily limited to) race, religion, ethnicity, gender, sexual orientation, nationality, age or generation, job function, and so on. Diversity is not limited to visible, physical differences. Inclusion is the act of understanding how those differences intersect and interact in group settings and ensuring that the differences are valued, respected, and understood. Inclusion is impossible without equity.

There is a popular image showing three children trying to view a baseball game over a fence (Figure 5.1). In the first picture, there is not level ground, and even though each child has the same size box, only one child can see the game. Here, each child is treated equally but not equitably. In the second picture, the children who were at a disadvantage are provided what they need to create equity. The third image shows the barrier (fence) completely removed and the ground level. This allows for **liberation**, defined as removing the barriers and inequities in the social systems that oppress or marginalize specific groups of people who share similar identities.

Even though "equity" has been more commonly used in the not-for-profit and social justice arenas before more recently gaining momentum in the corporate world, it remains an unclear term even in those areas with more experience using it.

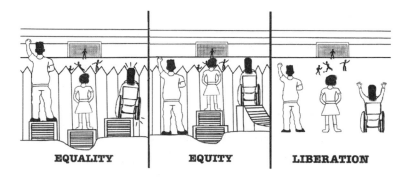

FIGURE 5.1 Equity versus Equality
Source: Created by The Winters Group, Inc., Krystle Nicholas artist.

A 2016 article in the *Stanford Social Innovation Review* written for the philanthropic community asserts that "the term 'equity' is spreading like wildfire in some philanthropic circles. It is showing up more and more in organizations' mission and values statements. It is making its way into the titles of conferences, plenary and breakout sessions, and meetings at the national, state, and local levels. Equity is one of those terms that everyone seems to understand at some visceral level, but few people share the same definition."[1]

If equity is the path to achieving inclusion and belonging, we have to start with equitable conversations. We cannot have equitable conversations if we cannot even agree on the definition of the word. The questions to ask about equity in preparing for inclusive conversations include: Are we assuming that everyone can see the ball game? What are the different needs that we should consider to ensure that the condition of equity is met? The conditions for an equitable conversation include:

1. A clear definition of equity.

2. Recognition of your power position in the conversation.

3. A deep understanding of where the person of lesser power is positioned and how that influences the impact and outcome of the conversation.

4. Exploration of what it would take to create an equitable environment for an inclusive conversation by giving **agency** (power to people to think and act to shape their experiences) to those in lesser power positions.

Power

Power differences can make it difficult to have an equitable conversation. Consider a conversation between a white male manager and an African American female direct report. The direct report has asked for the conversation because she feels that she is not being treated fairly. Two of her male colleagues have been promoted over her in the past two years, and she feels that her race and gender are the reasons she has been passed over. It is a male-dominated organization. The manager holds power as a male and as a leader. He should acknowledge his power in the situation and attempt to create a space where his direct report will have equal voice.

If you are the white male manager, engage in metacognitive thinking. Ask yourself: Why has this African American female direct report not been promoted? What skills is she lacking? Have I told her what they are? Do we have a plan in place for her to enhance those skills? If I cannot point to any deficiencies in her performance, do I have biases? If I was really honest with myself, what are some of those biases? Why is it that the entire leadership team is male? Do I think that she would not fit because in and out of work we have a kind of camaraderie that might make her and us uncomfortable? What do I know about how African American women fare at this company and in the work world in general? Are there systemic biases? Am I really going to work with her to help her achieve her goals? Explore research such as the study referenced in Chapter 1, conducted by McKinsey and LeanIn.org. The findings are that women of color are less likely to have managers who promote their work contributions and specifically that African American women do not get the same type of support to help them navigate organizational politics; also their managers are less likely to socialize with them outside of work.[2] The result is that more often than not women of color are excluded from informal networks that are known to enhance career upward mobility.

If you are the African American woman, your thinking might include: What tangible contributions can I point to that exceeded expectations? Was I recognized for those achievements? What specific instances can I cite where my contributions were not acknowledged? Did my manager perceive the results to be above average? Are there deficiencies in my performance that I am overlooking? How likely is it that my manager will agree with my assessment? Is the "male" culture so entrenched that he has blind spots that may preclude him from seeing the difference in how I am treated? What are my choices if I don't get the support that I need?

The meeting might start with dialogue like this:

DIRECT REPORT (AFRICAN AMERICAN WOMAN): As I mentioned when I requested this meeting, I want to discuss my career progress and better understand the steps I need to take so that I am given consideration when the next opportunity arises.

MANAGER (WHITE MALE): I am happy to talk with you, and I recognize that as your supervisor I have a lot to do with these decisions. By virtue of my position, power dynamics can stymie open and honest discussions. I want to acknowledge that and ask what you need in this discussion to feel that you are being listened to. What can I do to create a space where you feel that your perspective is just as important as mine?

DIRECT REPORT: This is not an easy conversation, and I appreciate you recognizing that. The conditions that will work for me are that you listen for understanding and not just to respond, and you acknowledge that societal discrimination and unconscious biases are real and may impact outcomes for people like me differently than for your identity, especially in the organizational culture that has primarily been run by men.

MANAGER: I promise to try to listen without judgment and to hear what you are saying. While it might be hard, I don't want you to think about me as the boss but rather a trusted adviser who is listening to understand. With that, I will ask clarifying questions that might seem obvious to you but perhaps not so much to me. I would like you to assume that I have positive intent and am trying to enhance my understanding of your perspective. I also want you to feel comfortable pointing out the unintended impact that I may be having on you.

Being open, upfront about the fact that the power dynamics make equitable conversations difficult, sets up a greater likelihood that a brave space is being created.

The Complexities of Power

Power dynamics need to be considered for successful inclusive conversations as was attempted in the dialogue above. There is individual positional power and there is also systemic power defined earlier. In the scenario above both types of power are present. The boss has a role in the organization that affords him the power to make decisions about the career progression of those who report to him. He is also a member of an identity group (white male) that has historically enjoyed unearned privilege. The sociological concepts of dominant and subordinated groups help us understand systemic power dynamics.

Dominant groups are those with systemic power, privileges, and social status within a society. Conversely subordinated groups are those that have been traditionally/historically oppressed, excluded, or disadvantaged in society. Dominant groups are considered the norm and by default subordinated groups are considered "abnormal"; dominant groups make the rules, and all others are judged by their standards (Table 5.1).[3] Dominance and subordination are not equivalent to majority and minority. Consider Apartheid in South Africa. Blacks were the numerical majority; even so, whites were the dominant group with the power.

It is important to note that we can hold power and privilege in one of our identity groups and be subordinated in another. For example, as a cisgender, heterosexual woman, I am part of a dominant group, whereas someone who identifies as a part of the LGBTQ community is a member of a subordinated group.

TABLE 5.1 Dominant Groups and Subordinated Groups

Dominant Groups	Subordinated Groups
Considered the norm or default	Seen as different, deviant from the norm
Benefit from the status quo	Expected to assimilate to status quo
Typically unaware of group membership (privilege)	Aware of group membership (oppression)
Make the rules	Must follow or adapt to rules
Access to power, resources	Barriers to access, resources
Benefit of doubt	Suspected

Source: Based on Louise Diamond, "Dominant and Subordinate Group Membership," Alliance for Peacebuilding.

There are still twenty-six states and three territories that do not have legislation banning employment discrimination against the LGBTQ community, and there is no federal legislation.[4] Conversely, my identity as a Black woman makes me a part of a historically subordinated group.

In one of The Winters Group experiential exercises to help participants understand power, we ask them to consider the identities that they shared in the "What Is My Identity" exercise described in detail in Chapter 3 and select those where they have a dominant position. Participants are asked to stand next to the chart of one of the identities. Others who share privilege in that same identity form a group and are asked to explore these questions:

1. How am I viewed as a member of this group?

2. How do I experience belonging?

3. When am I aware of my group membership?

4. How do I experience power as a member of this group?

5. What "rules" have been advantageous to me as a member of this group?

6. In what ways might my group be contributing to systemic inequity?

7. How can I use my social power to advance diversity, equity, and inclusion?

I recently participated in a poverty simulation that reminded me of the privileges I enjoy as a part of the middle class. As an example of how systems of power and privilege continue to disadvantage, the simulation highlights the systemic obstacles that people face on a day-to-day basis in their attempts to provide for their families and improve their economic situation. For instance, if the only way you can apply for a particular service is if you have transportation, and you rely on public transportation that is unreliable in your area, it may mean that by the time you arrive at the office to apply, it is closed. If you cannot afford childcare, you may have limited ability to follow up on job opportunities. The simulation demonstrates that no matter how hard one might try, systems may be unwittingly or intentionally set up to disadvantage you. The coronavirus pandemic magnified the differences between the "haves" and the "have-nots" that contributed to a disproportionate number of deaths of Black people in the United States.

Think about those identities where you are the dominant group—the group that is considered the norm—and answer the questions posed above. We cannot have inclusive conversations without considering power and privilege. The curious thing about power is that it may make us more prone to bias and stereotyping and less likely to be empathetic—one of the conditions for inclusive conversations that I describe in Chapter 8.

Research by Dr. Jeremy Hogeveen, Michael Inzlicht, and Sukhvinder Obhi goes as far as to say that power changes the way the brain responds to others.[5] In their studies of brain wave changes the researchers found that powerful people are more apt to stereotype, less likely to listen to the perspectives of the less powerful, and are less empathetic. They concluded that this could explain the tendency for the powerful to neglect the powerless, and the tendency for the powerless to expend so much effort in understanding the powerful. Inclusive conversations have to acknowledge the inequities that may be inherent based on the dominant and subordinated positions of those pursuing the dialogue.

The example of the boss (a white man) and the direct report (an African American woman) provides guidance for one-to-one conversation where power needs to be acknowledged. If it is a group dialogue, consider these questions in metacognitive self-talk: Am I aware of my power? Who is in the power position in the conversation? If it is me, how will I share my power? Am I stereotyping? Am I able to be empathetic? How do I acknowledge my power in an inclusive way? If I am not in the power position, questions might include: Do I feel that my voice will be heard? What are my triggers that might impact my ability to engage in this conversation? What biases do I have about those who are in the dominant/power position? Here are some possible ways to equalize power in a team conversation:

> Acknowledge and discuss the concepts of dominant and subordinated group dynamics before the conversation so that participants are aware of these realities.

> Be explicit that the intent is to create a space for equitable dialogue.

> Develop equitable conditions by asking each person in the group what needs to happen for them to feel heard during this conversation.

> Allow the person/people in the subordinated position to talk first.

> Give those in a subordinated position more air-time.

> Call out perspectives that uphold dominant societal norms and narratives, as well as those that minimize or dismiss subordinated group perspectives.

Practice **multipartiality**, which is defined as an empathetic openness and the ability to integrate opposing perspectives and models in dialogue. Strategies to attain multipartiality in inclusive conversations include:

> Identify the goal: "The goal of this conversation is to…"

> Combat binaries using "both/and" instead of narratives or arguments that suggest "either/or."

> Call out the gaps by asking, "Who or what community is *not* a part of this conversation? Why?" For example, if you are on a committee that is discussing new policies for dress codes in school, are parents a part of the conversation? If your organization is conducting an engagement survey, do you include the voices of the DEI practitioners as to what questions to include on the organization's inclusive practices?

> Redirect from dominant narratives by asking, "Does anyone have a different experience from those shared?" Sometimes

those from historically excluded groups do not offer their perspective when it is obviously different from that of the dominant group that holds the power.

> Be prepared to share unrepresented experiences using narrative, video, guest speakers, and so on.

> Clarify what is at stake: "If we do not consider the experiences of [underrepresented group], then…"

Power can either thwart or enhance our ability to have inclusive conversations. It depends on how we use it. If we acknowledge it and strive for equity, it is clearly an enhancer. If we are oblivious to it, or wield it in ways to continue to subordinate others, power obstructs any attempts to engage in inclusive conversations.

━━━━━━━━━ SUMMARY ━━━━━━━━━

> Inclusive conversations, by definition, must be equitable conversations.

> Equity is giving people what they need and deserve. Equality is giving everyone the same regardless of need.

> We cannot have equitable conversations without naming the power dynamics.

> Create brave spaces to discuss equity and power.

> Dominant groups are those with systemic power, privileges, and social status within a society. Conversely subordinated groups are those that have been traditionally/historically oppressed, excluded, or disadvantaged in society.

> The power afforded to dominant groups is not necessarily earned or wanted. It is not their fault that they have it. It is,

however, crucial to acknowledge it and use it to dismantle the inequitable systems.

Discussion/Reflection Questions

1. In what ways do you distinguish equality and equity? What systems in your organization are based on an equality-versus-equity framework?

2. What are some ways to move from equity to liberation?

3. Where is your power? Is it positional? Dominant group?

4. On a day-to-day basis, how do you include historically subordinated voices?

5. How do you use your power to dismantle inequitable systems?

-{ SIX }-

Face Fear and Fragility

Fear and fragility are inextricably connected. The history of cross-difference dynamics—whether it be race, religion, ethnicity, sexual orientation, gender, socioeconomics, or other aspects of our identity—have left our society psychologically scarred, scared, and stuck in a vicious web of denial, defensiveness, and intergenerational trauma that is often too painful to even talk about.

Defining Fear

It is against this backdrop of a sordid and painful history that we are asking dominant and subordinated groups to come together and talk about our differences. Why wouldn't there be fear and fragility? As an identifiable (based on my skin color) African American woman, I carry a certain amount of fear with me on a daily basis. "Living while Black" for people of color means that you are always on guard, especially in unfamiliar surroundings. How will my skin color impact how I am going to be treated? Based on lived experiences too numerous to even begin to share, I have learned to be cautious and attuned when I am in spaces where I don't see other people of color. It is not always to the level of "fear" as defined in this chapter, but there is a certain level of anxiety. Among my family and circle of friends, questions routinely asked are: Do you think there will be other Black people there? How are Black people treated there?

Karl Albrecht, an author and management consultant, defines fear as an anxious feeling, caused by our anticipation of an imagined event or experience.[1] He explains that there are five basic fears, from which all other so-called "fears" emanate.[2] These are (1) extinction or death; (2) mutilation or losing a body part; (3) loss of autonomy—being immobilized, paralyzed, restricted, entrapped, imprisoned, smothered, or otherwise controlled by circumstances beyond our control; (4) separation—abandonment, rejection, and loss of connectedness, or not being wanted, respected, or valued by others; and (5) ego-death—humiliation, shame, or any other mechanism of profound self-disapproval that threatens the integrity of the self. Fear that is manifested by loss of autonomy, separation, and/or ego-death resonate as we think about inclusion, equity, and belonging.

Societal Fear

There are troubling signs that the world is again embracing ideologies of separation from those who are different veiled as nationalism and patriotism. **Populism**, a political approach that strives to appeal to ordinary people who feel that their concerns are disregarded by established elite groups, is on the rise. This ideology uses xenophobic paranoia and a rejection of any form of global cooperation in favor of a strong, country-first approach to international affairs.[3]

This trend is fueled largely by fear—fear of loss of autonomy—the sense of being trapped by something that is beyond one's control. There is a fear that immigrants and other "minorities" will destroy the dominant culture's way of life; they will take over, leaving "us" powerless. Recent elections around the world of populist regimes contribute to anti-inclusion messages. Right-wing populist and nationalist governments are in power in Brazil, Hungary, India, Israel, Philippines, Poland, Russia, Turkey, and the United States, among other countries. Experts in the United States think that Donald Trump won the presidency in 2016 because the Democrats paid little attention to economically vulnerable white people. Even though technology is largely to blame for upending the need for many entry-level unskilled jobs that are now automated, job loss and personal economic decline is attributed to foreigners and **affirmative action**. The fear manifests in statements like "They are taking our jobs."

While dominant group fear is based on loss of autonomy, the fear among targeted groups is based on what Albrecht describes as separation and ego-death fear. We should not minimize the dire effects these types of fears have on children during their formative years. The sense of abandonment and rejection simply because of one's identity will in many cases lead to psychological issues in adulthood. Think about the impact on migrant children who are in detention centers separated from their parents because of strict immigration policies.

At the extreme, fear plays out in the escalating violence that we see globally. Mass shootings as well as destruction of churches, temples, and mosques are much more commonplace today. Extremist groups are coming from the underground to the forefront, spewing hate and messages of their supremacy. Hate crimes are on the rise around the world. Our fears of those who are different play a major role in limiting our ability for inclusive conversations.

Identity-Based Trauma

These current-day traumatic experiences faced by a disproportionate number of historically subordinated groups increase the
chances of identity-based trauma. "Trauma" is defined by the
American Psychological Association (APA) as "an emotional
response to a terrible event like an accident, rape or natural disaster." The APA describes the impact like this: "Immediately
after the event, shock and denial are typical. Longer term reactions include unpredictable emotions, flashbacks, strained relationships and even physical symptoms like headaches or nausea.
I don't think these feelings are normal. Not sure what I meant
there."[4]

Most of us are familiar with the term Post-Traumatic Stress
Disorder (PTSD). It is usually a condition associated with mil-
itary combat veterans. The US Department of Veteran Affairs
defines PTSD as "a mental health problem that some people
develop after experiencing or witnessing a life-threatening event,
like combat, a natural disaster, a car accident, or sexual assault."[5]
Identity-based trauma has not been as widely researched or talked
about, but it is just as real as other traumas that people may face
today, according to Nnamdi Pole, PhD, professor of clinical psychology at Smith College. Pole contends that the psychological
impact of racial injustices can lead to PTSD.[6] He says that the re-
peated images of Black people being assaulted by police can cause
trauma for young Black men in particular and all Black people
in general, even when they have not personally experienced the
event. Just knowing that you belong to an identity group where
there may be potential harm increases the chances of trauma.

Identity-based trauma is also more likely to manifest as
Pre-Traumatic Stress Syndrome, which refers to the anticipation

and fear that come with knowing that you might be targeted just because of who you are. As defined in a 2017 news report: "The symptoms are similar to post-traumatic stress disorder (including grief, sadness, worry, disturbing intrusive thoughts, sleep troubles and nightmares, and avoiding situations or activities that are reminiscent of the stressful event), but in this case, they stem from anticipatory anxiety about an event that may occur in the future."[7]

Social scientists have coined the term "historical trauma" to refer to the multigenerational, communal trauma that oppressed and marginalized groups have faced.[8] For example, when Black people see the brutal attacks against Black people in the media, it is reminiscent of a long history of brutality (e.g., lynching) toward Black people in this country. When Jewish people witness their synagogues being attacked by white supremacists today, this brings back memories of the Holocaust and other injustices targeted toward Jewish people. In the current sociopolitical climate, a number of identities are under attack. Inclusive conversations are hindered by identity-based trauma that may not even be conscious to the victims. This type of trauma can impede our ability for intercultural trust, discussed in Chapter 8.

Trauma and Perpetrators of Identity-Based Violence

There is also a theory that it is not only the victims of identity-based violence who experience trauma but also the perpetuators. **Perpetration-Induced Traumatic Stress (PITS)**, a term coined by peace psychologist Rachel MacNair, describes incidents of PTSD resulting from the trauma of having committed violence, as contrasted with trauma caused by witnessing or being the recipient of a violent act.[9] PITS plays out as shock and denial. The theory is that white America is so overwhelmed by its history of injustice that it has gone into deep denial. Shock and denial are aspects of **white fragility,** a concept advanced by Robin DiAngelo, which I elaborate on later in this chapter.[10]

The psychological ramifications of the trauma that people of color and other marginalized groups face as victims and that white people face as perpetrators emanate from deep fear of the other.

According to experts, fear and trauma weaken the immune system, which can lead to cardiovascular damage, gastrointestinal problems such as ulcers and irritable bowel syndrome, and decreased fertility. Fear and trauma can also lead to accelerated aging and even premature death.[11]

Actions to Mitigate Fear

Analyze fears using metacognitive approaches. If the fear-induced situation is not putting you in imminent danger, ask yourself: Why am I so afraid? What evidence do I have that my fear is valid? If you are a person from a marginalized identity group that literally holds fear as a regular way of being, it is important to name it, analyze it, and do something about it, like seek professional help. Often, one may not associate physical and emotional symptoms with fear. It may manifest as depression, fatigue, heightened anxiety, and other diseases such as high blood pressure, diabetes, and mental disorders. Another problem: studies show that people of color are less likely to seek mental health solutions as there is often a cultural stigma attached.

Share your fear with a trusted friend or colleague. Talking about our fears can be very cathartic. Tell someone you trust about why you are afraid and ask them to listen and offer their perspective.

Face your fears head on. Behavioral scientists say that if we are able to experience situations where we confront our fears, these experiences can serve to quell our fears because we may find that they are unfounded. For example, for many years I was afraid of dogs because as a child I was attacked by one. Putting myself in situations with dogs over the years has mitigated that fear. If you fear an identity group other than your own, for instance, intentionally having more contact with that group can decrease your sense of fear. You might start by watching documentaries or reading books that provide an accurate perspective. After that you might genuinely reach out to engage with a co-worker who is different.

Resist believing stereotypical representations of groups. The saying "don't believe everything you hear" is really good advice in this day of rapid-fire communication that technology makes possible. Watching the daily news and staying on your social media feeds can induce unfounded anxiety and fear. When you hear or see these stories, ask yourself: What emotion did this cause me to have? Why? Does it fuel fear based on negative stereotypes of a group?

Addressing Fears in Team Settings

When fear is present in team dynamics, any hope to reap the advantages that come from teamwork are thwarted. The power of teamwork, the bringing together of diverse ideas and experiences, has the potential to create better solutions than any one individual can do on their own. The following ideas are ways to address fear in teams:

> **Model behavior.** If you are the leader, model behavior by showing vulnerability and that it is okay to make mistakes. Mistakes show that learning is happening. Keep in mind, as pointed out in Chapter 4, that making mistakes may be riskier for historically subordinated groups, so be mindful of biases or double standards.

> **Assess team dynamics.** Who contributes in team meetings and who does not? Understand why and how each person might like to engage by building individual relationships with team members. In addition to reducing fear, this action can build trust.

> **Practice equity not equality.** As pointed out in Chapter 5, equity means that you provide support based on differing levels of needs. Make sure the team understands the concept of equity and it is not seen as "charity" or preferential treatment that looks like favoritism. For example, giving more time to a newer team member to catch up is equity not preferential treatment. If English is not a team member's first language, make sure to send out meeting documents well in advance to give time for comprehension.

> **Understand that words matter.** Be intentional in word choices so that you are not promulgating fear and intimidation. Chapter 11 explores this in more detail.

Understanding Fragility

Fear and fragility are related. Fear can induce fragility, and by the same token fragility can lead to fear. The word "fragility" and its root word "fragile" are often associated with the need to be "careful" or "gentle" with a subject. "Fragility" suggests a certain degree of delicacy, thereby requiring more effort in handling whatever or whomever it is because you are fearful that if you do not apply such delicate handling, an unwanted outcome might happen. "White fragility," a term coined by sociologist Robin DiAngelo and articulated in her best-selling book by the same name, is defined as a state in which even a minimum amount of racial stress becomes intolerable, triggering a range of defensive moves on the part of white people. These moves include the outward display of emotions such as anger, fear, and guilt, and behaviors such as argumentation, silence, and leaving the stress-inducing situation. These behaviors, in turn, function to reinstate white racial dominance.[12]

Brittany J. Harris, vice president of Learning and Innovation at The Winters Group, recounted a story in *The Inclusion Solution*, The Winters Group blog and newsletter, about how a middle-schooler was eloquently able to name white fragility. Brittany is a member of a curriculum advisory board for an urban school district. The board chose to engage a student, a Black girl in the seventh grade, in the curriculum review to provide feedback as a student.

When asked her thoughts and what she would recommend, the student offered a youthful articulation of white fragility. She wanted the board to make sure that when they experienced the assignments and discussed the articles (one of which explored the impact of redlining, gentrification, and modern-day segregation in urban cities) that "the teachers not make the few white students in the class feel badly about their ancestors." She didn't want the white students to "be sad or get offended."

Without knowing it, this young person had explained white fragility—and the ways in which it showed up in her world. Brittany said that it was a powerful moment in that room with teachers, curriculum designers, and other board members (people in power). This Black student studying within an urban, underfunded school system, living within a socioeconomically, disenfranchised community, still felt compelled to center the feelings of white students when sharing what she wanted to see in the curriculum.

What If We Acknowledged Black (Marginalized Group) Fragility?

What if we turned the concept on its head to talk about Black fragility and defined it in terms of vulnerability, the quality or state of being exposed to the possibility of being attacked or harmed, either physically or emotionally. What if we thought about the extra care that historically marginalized groups need because we have intergenerational trauma from our own painful history? Perhaps if we believed in Black fragility we would not have underfunded urban schools, disparities in educational outcomes, disproportionate numbers of people of color who are incarcerated, vast socioeconomic disparities, and representation inequities in the workforce. If we believed in Black fragility, maybe we would not find concepts like equity to be controversial because we would easily see that everybody is not getting what they need and deserve. If we embraced Black fragility, we would not be chastised for calling the "race card." As a matter of fact, we would be invited to do so.

Some of the response to DiAngelo's work by people of color is that we don't have the privilege of being fragile. We have to be tough and not show any vulnerability. For example, I was taught: "You can't show white people any weakness because they will use it against you." "Be strong" is a common refrain in communities of color, acknowledging just how difficult it is to succeed in the midst of oppressive systems. However, under the "be strong" veneer is a type of unspoken fragility that eats away at our very being. Suppressing our fragility leads to fatigue that in turn leads to dire psychological and physical health consequences.

Is Resilience Too Much to Ask?

"Resilience" is another buzz word gaining in popularity in the DEI space. As defined in *Merriam-Webster*, "resilience" is "the ability to mentally or emotionally cope with a crisis or to return to pre-crisis status quickly." It is a lot to ask to bounce back *quickly* from some of the injustices that induce fear and trauma. The systems that promulgate inequities did not happen quickly, and I daresay we cannot recover quickly. A "get over it," "grin and bear it," "keep a stiff upper lip" attitude suggests that there is little need to talk about it, unpack the situation, be with the normal emotions that might be associated with the trauma and/or seek professional help if needed. The Winters Group conducted an informal online survey in December 2019 asking respondents to share how working in DEI impacts their emotional, physical, and mental health. Here are a few of the representative responses:

> ❯ The emotional toll: It has made me numb. The mental toll: It has robbed my sleep and made me paranoid. My physical health: Blood clots and circulation issues from flights all over the world for the company.

> Since taking on a full-time diversity and inclusion (D&I) role in mid-2019, I oftentimes have a need to escape and unplug from the toll and emotional tax of the work we do.

> Now I recognize that this work is a lot more intense and draining than I was expecting. Some challenges include feeling like a failure when I am not able to impact systemic change, and instead am asked to work within a box; or the pressure I feel to always exemplify cultural competence and inclusive leadership (I'm in the spotlight).

> I often feel misunderstood, alone, and confused at work, especially when I am the only one who appears to recognize bias as it unfolds.

> As a white person leading DEI work at an incredibly diverse organization, I am constantly asked, "Why are YOU leading this work?" Like for everyone who has to consistently justify their validity, it's emotionally exhausting. And it's ironic since the whole purpose of DEI work is to lessen people's need to justify their presence or the validity of their perspectives.

> As a woman of color, I initially fell into this work. At every job, regardless of title, I created a diversity component that was incorporated into the company. It wasn't by choice, but rather by necessity! Often there were barriers and misunderstandings. Mentally, I am tougher and more knowledgeable and quite comfortable "speaking truth to power." I'm also focused and determined. Emotionally, I am fragile....I have to channel the emotions, the sadness, the rage at what shouldn't be and what I must work to change.

> I am a nervous wreck. I've gained twenty pounds since early spring. I've been in the role for two years and quite suddenly I became very bad at it, though none of my job actions and activities changed. I feel like I'm under a microscope and that my every error is magnified times twenty. Because I had quite long honeymoon in this job, I made the mistake of feeling and being free to bring my authentic self to the office. Not a smart move.

While resilience is important, it will not change the system. It merely allows us to more effectively cope with the status quo.

The fear and fragility associated with DEI work is significant. It takes quite an emotional and even physical toll. We need to acknowledge that more, have inclusive conversations about how to manage the fear and fragility, and be careful in advocating resilience as a solution. Self-care is extremely important in DEI work, especially in engaging in inclusive conversations that are likely to induce triggers and anxiety. Knowing when to unplug, take some "me time," and/or seek professional support is critical.

SUMMARY

> There is a lot of cross-difference fear, some of it based on our history and some based on today's global sociopolitical climate. Dominant group and subordinated group fear of the "other" manifest in different ways.

> Inclusive conversations are not possible if fear is present. To address fears, we have to be willing to name them, analyze the root cause, and face them head on.

> Fear and fragility are related. White fragility keeps us from having meaningful conversations about race. It can actually stop them before they even start.

> Historically marginalized groups are fragile too, but that fragility is not often acknowledged intragroup or by other groups.

> We have to create brave spaces to talk about fear and fragility.

> We should be careful in advocating "resilience" alone as the solution to the fear and trauma associated with DEI work.

Discussion/Reflection Questions

1. What are your fears of engaging in conversations with identity groups different from you?

2. What are some ways to mitigate the fears?

3. How does white fragility show up for you? In your organization?

4. How might injustices for historically marginalized groups be mitigated if we acknowledged marginalized group fragility?

5. What does resilience mean to you? How can you be resilient while at the same time attend to the toll that DEI work can take?

-(**SEVEN**)-

Extend Grace and Forgiveness

> For inclusive conversations, the heart must have the desire for grace and forgiveness, the head must know the nature of grace and forgiveness, and the hand must know the path to achieve it.

Almost every day some high-profile person is called out in the media for saying or doing something that is considered insensitive or racist. Consider the comedian Kevin Hart's despicable homophobic jokes from 2012 that were brought to light on Twitter and the controversy that ensued about whether that transgression should ban him from hosting the 2019 Oscars. Ultimately he did not host, even though he apologized many times and said that he had learned a lot since he made those remarks.

Many were outraged when Fox News host Megyn Kelly was dismissive about displaying blackface. Actor Rosanne Barr lost her starring role in her own TV sitcom for racist remarks against top Obama adviser Valerie Jarrett. A Rochester, New

York, meteorologist was fired in 2019 for saying Martin Luther "Coon" instead of Martin Luther King. He immediately corrected his faux pas on air. The Rev. Bernice King, daughter of the famed civil rights leader, said she does not think the weatherman should have been fired.[1] Instead, she called for repercussions including an apology but thought the firing went too far. US Representative Steve King (Republican from Iowa) was admonished by both parties for his remarks in a *New York Times* interview: "White nationalist, white supremacist, Western civilization—how did that language become offensive?"[2] As punishment he was stripped of all committee assignments. He says his statements were mischaracterized, but he has a long history of making comments about Muslims, immigrants, and other nonwhite groups.

Does Everyone Deserve Forgiveness?

Some offenders seem genuinely contrite and their apologics sincere—"I just did not know" or "I did not mean it," in the case of the meteorologist. Others appear to be dismissive and downplay the impact of their actions as no big deal (Megyn Kelly). How can we really know who is sincere with their apologies? Does everyone deserve forgiveness? Steve King appears to hold deep-seated and long-standing racist views. Even if we forgive, should there be irrevocable consequences for the actions? For example, should Kevin Hart never be able to host the Oscars? What is the right punishment? Should losing one's job or source of income always be the solution? Who gets to decide the punishment?

These are obviously difficult questions with no one right answer where we would likely find widespread agreement. I contend that we have to include grace and forgiveness as one of the conditions for inclusive conversations. If our standard solution to diversity, equity, and inclusion (DEI) infractions is punishment, case closed, let's move on without the opportunity for conversation, we don't learn. If we don't learn, we don't make progress toward equity, empathy, and belonging.

The concepts of grace and forgiveness related to engaging in inclusive conversations are the most complex to unpack and provide practical solutions, perhaps because they are rooted in theology and therefore engender many different beliefs. The definition of forgiveness may differ somewhat from religion to religion, but all have some notion of letting go of the hurt someone has caused you, even if they are not deserving (grace). Outside of religious teachings, psychologists define forgiveness similarly as a conscious, deliberate decision to release feelings of resentment or vengeance toward a person or group who has harmed you, regardless of whether they actually deserve your forgiveness. Grace and forgiveness do not mean forgetting, nor do they mean condoning or excusing offenses.[3]

Forgiveness allows us to extend grace, unearned consideration. Spiritual leaders and behavioral scientists remind us that forgiveness is more for the victim than the perpetrator. It frees us from the anger and hurt that keeps us from moving forward. Deep-seated anger and hurt can inhibit our ability to have inclusive conversations.

Why Are Grace and Forgiveness Important for Inclusive Conversations?

In theological terms, grace is extending kindness to the unworthy and forgiveness is letting go of hurt and pain caused by another. These two related conditions are needed for inclusive conversations because we still live in a world where we woefully lack knowledge and understanding of the experiences of different identity groups, as illustrated with some of the examples at the beginning of the chapter. Even the most well-informed people will make mistakes about DEI-related subjects. If we do not extend grace and forgiveness, we will never get to the real inclusive conversations. If we fear being punished for saying or doing something wrong, chances are we will just remain silent.

Learning to "call people in" to a conversation rather than "calling them out" to embarrass or punish is a condition for inclusive conversations. Calling people in does not mean that what they said or did is okay; it simply means that we initially assume positive intent and engage in conversation to better understand why they did or said it and share the impact of their behavior. Their response will largely determine if grace and forgiveness, or some other action, are appropriate.

Today we live in what has been dubbed a **cancel culture**, where it is common to call people out. Usually linked to social media, this means public shaming of someone (usually a celebrity) who has said something that is considered insensitive, racist, homophobic, sexist, or otherwise offensive. Some argue that celebrities deserve to be canceled after problematic actions or words; others believe the punishment doesn't always fit the "crime." Regarding DEI wrongdoings, we are slow to forgive and quick to seek punishment. Egregious infractions such as hate crimes certainly deserve punishment. However, there are a lot of "wrongs" that are simply out of lack of understanding and knowledge for which we can extend grace and forgiveness.

Writer and cultural critic Kimberly Foster says in the video *We Can't Cancel Everyone*: "Changing culture meaningfully means approaching folks from the standpoint of 'these harmful ideas you are perpetuating need to go.' We're not going to accept this anymore. But the people themselves can be recovered."[4] We need grace and forgiveness so that we can recover to engage in meaningful conversations that lead to equity, empathy, and belonging. One of The Winters Group's university clients has established a norm for student discussions allowing them to ask for "space and grace" to discuss difficult diversity topics.

Grace and Forgiveness Include Acknowledgment and Accountability

Grace and forgiveness are tall orders, especially when the offense tears at the very core of an individual's or a group's identity. We should hold the perpetrators accountable. However, harboring feelings of anger and hostility toward those who have caused pain is not good for our physical or mental health. Studies show that forgiveness can improve health, lowering the risk of heart attack; improving cholesterol levels and sleep; and reducing pain, blood pressure, and levels of anxiety, depression, and stress.[5]

Miroslav Volf, professor of theology at Yale University, in his book *Free of Charge: Giving and Forgiving in a Culture Stripped of Grace*, contends that forgiveness is not without accountability.[6] He maintains that we should name the wrong act and condemn the doer. However, he also asserts that the motivation for calling out the wrong act should not be for vengeance or to punish. While he is not saying that punishment is not warranted nor that justice should not be sought, forgiveness should be based on the desire to right the wrong and rebuild relationships. This perspective is especially important in service of enabling inclusive conversations. South African Archbishop Desmond Tutu and his daughter Mpho Tutu put it this way in *The Book of Forgiving: The Fourfold Path for Healing Ourselves and Our World:* "Forgiveness does not subvert justice—it creates space for justice to be enacted with a purity of purpose that does not include revenge."[7] Volf says that forgiveness is a social contract between parties and does not happen if only the offended is doing the forgiving. The offender must be remorseful and acknowledge their wrongdoing. He shares how difficult his advice is because it is hard to always know the extent to which someone has acted wrongfully and as humans we don't like to be blamed and might not agree with the offended.

Nelson Mandela provides a great example of grace, forgiveness, and accountability. After spending twenty-seven years in a South African prison on Robben Island for his activism against Apartheid, he used the approach of grace and forgiveness to work toward reconciliation. South Africa's Truth and Reconciliation Commission aimed to ensure individual accountability through the disclosure of the identities of all perpetrators and their crimes, along with public shaming and the promise of an apology, as well as the eventual prosecutions of perpetrators who did not apply for amnesty. The mantra was "there is a need for understanding but not for vengeance, a need for reparation but not for retaliation, a need for ubuntu (humanity) but not for victimization."[8]

The families of the nine worshippers who were killed by an avowed white supremist in 2016 in Charleston, South Carolina, said they forgave Dylann Roof for this horrible hate crime for which he has shown no remorse.[9] In 2019 the brother of Botham Jean, the Black man who was shot and killed in Dallas by a white female police officer who claimed she mistook his apartment for hers, asked the judge at the sentencing if he could hug her. He said, "I forgive you."[10] One of the survivors of the Christchurch New Zealand mosque shooting in 2019 also expressed forgiveness. "Maybe he was lost, maybe he has made a mistake," said Mohan Ibn Ibrahm, who was at the Masjid Al-Noor at the time of the shooting.[11]

Perpetrators of hate crimes surely deserve their due punishment. They must be held accountable. And we must not misinterpret forgiveness in these situations as a "get out of jail free pass," a reason to minimize, dismiss, or forget the impact—now we can move on with no collective responsibility because the victims have forgiven us. I am not suggesting that forgiveness should be assumed or demanded in these extreme or even lessor offenses. However, I believe that at the very least the spirit of grace and forgiveness is needed to move forward. Tutu has said that if South Africa had taken a vengeance approach, it would have led to destruction rather than repair.

The Nature of Forgiving Conversations

Tutu and his daughter have asserted that forgiveness is a conversation and like most important conversations it needs language that is clear and honest and sincere. They acknowledge how difficult forgiveness is and offer this Fourfold Path of forgiving: tell your story for as long as you need to; name your hurts until they no longer pierce your heart; grant forgiveness when you are ready to let go of a past that cannot be changed; and renew or release the relationship as you choose.

The very path to grace and forgiveness constitutes an inclusive conversation. In the introduction I referenced a situation that happened in a cultural proficiency session with teachers in a public school system where one of the white participants shared her belief that Black parents do not care as much about their children's education. A Black teacher vehemently disagreed and an uncomfortable conversation ensued. In this scenario the Black teacher was angry and hurt and wanted to hold the white person accountable for her comment with at the very least an apology. The white teacher did not see a reason for an apology because she claimed that this was her observation based on the differences she experienced with Black and white parents. In that case, forgiveness is not an option based on Volf's theories, nor is it an inclusive conversation. If the white teacher admitted her wrongdoing, we might adapt the Tutus's steps of telling your stories and naming the harms. For example:

> Allow those who have been hurt to share their truths. They should start with the facts and then share how they made them feel.

> Accept your and others' feelings as valid.

> Listen to understand, not to defend or dispute.

> Do not try to fix the pain or deemphasize the harm.

> Practice empathy and humility for those sharing their stories.

> Don't engage in **Oppression Olympics** (equating others' pain with something that was painful for you).

> Practice multipartiality as described in Chapter 5.

> Recognize that forgiveness may not happen immediately or ever. Give it time.

It would be even more impactful if another white teacher exercised bravery and allyship and challenged her colleague's comment. More and more, historically marginalized groups voice that they are tired of always being the ones to challenge uninformed or ill-informed dominant group individuals. An ally might say something like this to the white teacher: "While your interpretation may be that Black parents don't care about their children's education based on your experience, I would invite you to do some self-reflection asking yourself if you really think that you have enough experience to generalize about a whole group, and if you would consider another narrative that provides the opposite interpretation—that Black parents care just as much as white parents about their children's education but well-entrenched complex inequitable socioeconomic systems influence behaviors and outcomes. If you accept that, we have some common ground to engage in conversation." In *We Can't Talk about That at Work,* I assert that inclusive conversations happen when the parties first reach common ground. What is it that we can all agree on?

CASE SITUATION:
Should We Have Forgiven and Extended Grace?

A large organization called me in as a result of an incident that happened in a training session conducted by another consultant. In the session a long-term, well-respected manager used the

N-word several times in asking the facilitator why it is okay for Blacks to use this word and not for whites. She said that her sons listen to and repeat the word used in rap music. Other employees were appalled that she used this word (actually said the word) during this session. When she was called on it at a break, her response was "feedback is a gift." She did not apologize and perhaps there was no evidence of humility. She was fired soon after the incident.

Most African Americans at the organization thought that this was the appropriate punishment, whereas most whites did not. It created a great deal of hurt feelings and polarization among the staff. It seemed that the major concern from the Black employees was her lack of apology. White employees felt that a reprimand and education was more appropriate given her positive history with the organization.

As Miroslav Volf contends, forgiveness does not happen without repentance. In this instance the offender was not willing to acknowledge her wrongdoing and therefore forgiveness was not possible, even if the offended want to extend it. If the offender was interested in better understanding the complexities of the N-word, she might have started an inclusive conversation like this: "I would like to confirm that we are in a brave space and I am going to lean into my discomfort in asking this question (shows humility). I would like to ask for grace and forgiveness if needed if I make a mistake." If others were still offended by how she delivered her inquiry, she may have handled it this way: "I apologize for offending you. That was not my intent. I acknowledge that I was wrong. I ask for your forgiveness and that we can continue the conversation so that I can learn."

I don't know if there was a teaching moment where this explanation was shared with the fired executive. However, in the best-case scenario she could have asked for grace and forgiveness about her ignorance and this could have been a transformative experience. Instead, it ended in worsening race relations at this organization and inflicting irrevocable damage. For inclusive conversations—an interpersonal interaction— forgiveness must involve the forgiver and the forgiven. Each plays a role. Forgiveness occurs when the forgiver is ready to let go and the forgiven acknowledges the harm they have caused. If the offender is not willing to admit the wrongdoing, we can still choose to forgive at the intrapersonal level to let go of the pain and hurt that can eat away at our well-being. However, there is likely little opportunity for an inclusive conversation in these instances.

Teaching Moment

Why can Black people use the N-word and white people cannot? Although there are several rationales, the two most compelling are that some in the Black community have reclaimed the word that was a term of oppression by whites for many years, as an intraracial term of endearment reserved for each other. It acknowledges that in our culture there are certain terms that certain groups should not say to cultures different from their own. Author and activist Ta-Nehisi Coates points this out and uses the example that he calls his wife "honey" but would not call other women by that name, or that his wife might use the B-word in conversation with her friends, but he would never use that word with women.[12] It is all about the relationship that exists between the parties. Because of the racial history in America, whites, even though perhaps not personally guilty, should honor that the N-word is off-limits for them. There are many "rules," written and unwritten, about what you don't say about or to a particular group if you are not a member of that group. This is one of them.

The Oops, Ouch, and Educate Conversation Model

A very simple tool developed by Leslie Aguilar in her book *Ouch! That Stereotype Hurts* to engage in conversations that offer grace and forgiveness is offered below.[13] "Ouch" is when someone says something that is insensitive to you, and "oops" is when you say something that is offensive to someone else. If you say something that is offensive, accept the feedback, acknowledge what happened by stating both your intent and the unintended impact, apologize, and adjust. An inclusive conversation might sound something like this:

Ouch Conversation

Start with an "I" statement. "I" statements focus on the impact that the action had on you. They avoid using "you" or accusatory language so as not to put the offender on the defensive.

BEHAVIOR: "You Asians are so smart."

FEELINGS: I am frustrated because this is a stereotype that I hear often, and it is of course not categorically true.

IMPACT: It may impact my ability to trust that you are really an ally for inclusion.

Oops Conversation Starter

ACCEPT: I appreciate you telling me. Thank you.

ACKNOWLEDGE: I did not mean to offend you, but I realize that I did.

APOLOGIZE: I am sorry I said/did that.

ADJUST: I will certainly remember this lesson and not do it again.

The offended offered the offender grace, and the offender took responsibility for their actions and offered an authentic apology. The key point here is that even if you did not intend to offend, or even if you do not agree with the offender, apologize because you could not possibly know the impact. As outlined earlier, forgiveness is possible only when the offender takes responsibility for their wrongdoing. Grace and forgiveness offer us a path for inclusive conversations that acknowledge that none of us is perfect and that our mistakes offered with genuine contrition help us grow and get us closer to achieving our goal of a more inclusive world.

—————————— SUMMARY ——————————

> Grace and forgiveness are needed for inclusive conversations because many of us lack knowledge and understanding of our cultural "others."

> If our only approach is to chastise and punish, we shut down the possibility of meaningful conversations.

> Forgiveness is not easy and cannot be assumed, dictated, or expected. It is a choice.

> Forgiveness does not mean that we forget the injustices that so many have endured as members of subordinated groups.

> Forgiveness frees us from the hurt and pain and allows healing.

> Grace is related to forgiveness. It is unearned merit allowing for space to make mistakes and for learning to take place.

> For inclusive conversations, forgiveness requires the person who offended to acknowledge their wrongdoing and apologize.

> Inclusive conversations are not likely possible if the offender is not willing to acknowledge their mistake. The offended, however, can still choose to forgive.

> Grace and forgiveness should be a part of ground rules when engaging in inclusive conversations.

Discussion/Reflection Questions

1. Do you think grace and forgiveness are important for inclusive conversations? Why? Why not?

2. What are your thoughts about cancel culture?

3. Are there certain groups that should be held to a higher standard (e.g., celebrities and others in the public domain), for whom grace and forgiveness should not be extended?

4. In the situation of hate crimes, why do you think the victims forgive? Does this diminish the sense of accountability?

EIGHT

Facilitate Trust and Empathy

> As we develop the capacity for empathy for one another, our ability to trust each other increases.

Some years ago, I was conducting research for a philanthropic organization that was interested in attracting more donors of color. In one impactful interview, an elderly Black woman in Florida summed up the issue of trust in this way: "Why are you interested in me and my money now. I don't know you. We have never even broken bread together." In other words, she did not trust the organization's motives and pointed out in her own way that she did not have a relationship with them. Trust is a *mandatory* ingredient for inclusive conversations. Building trust across different dimensions of diversity is complex. It is easier to trust people with whom you have an affinity—who you perceive to be more like you—with whom you have a relationship.

Research shows that we do not have meaningful conversations across difference. A study by the Public Religion Research Institute showed that 75 percent of whites responded that they have meaningful conversations only with whites. By the same token, 65 percent of Blacks and 46 percent of Latinos said that they have meaningful conversations only with those of their own cultural group.[1] If we are not having conversations across difference, it is certainly difficult to build relationships that build trust. Developing meaningful relationships across difference reduces the fear and anxiety, as discussed in Chapter 6, that is often associated with interacting with our "others." Contributing to the lack of trust for historically subordinated groups is a history of inhumane treatment. Even though some of this treatment is no longer legal, multigenerational memory and damage impedes the ability to create trusting cross-cultural relationships.

Historical Dehumanization and Discrimination Diminishes Trust

In the United States and across the globe people from dominant groups have a history of **"othering"**—colonizing or, at worst, dehumanizing and engaging in acts of genocide against those from subordinated groups. There are many examples across different cultural groups where such actions persisted (and continue to persist in too many cases) for hundreds of years, which has engendered intergenerational mistrust. Consider slavery and the Jim Crow South. Native American mistrust that comes from the taking of their land and the dismantling of their way of life. One major reason that there is a lack of trust between Christian Americans and Muslim Americans is the 9/11 terrorism attacks. Of course, there are many other historic examples, including the Holocaust, Apartheid in South Africa, violence against the LGBTQ community both in the United States and elsewhere, the forced relocation of Japanese Americans and Japanese immigrants to internment camps during World War II, and inhumane treatment of people with disabilities, just to name a few.

Today, we hear numerous incidents of people calling authorities on Muslim, Latinx, African American, and the LGBTQ community because they feel uncomfortable. If we are afraid of each other, how can we build trust to have inclusive conversations? How do you have inclusive conversations if there has been no intentional efforts at trust-building? A few ideas to consider:

> Understand the historical reasons why there may be a lack of trust.

> Don't assume that that there is trust during initial attempts at inclusive conversations.

> Start slowly as trust is built one interaction at a time.

> Demonstrate humility, authenticity, and empathy.

The Importance of Empathy in Building Trust

A common response to someone else's situation is "I know how you feel." Do you really? Is this simply an automatic response? If you really thought about it (engage metacognition and self-awareness), you would realize that you don't know how the other feels because you have not had that lived experience. Such a knee-jerk response might seem inauthentic to the other person and impede trust building. Empathy is the capacity to understand or feel what another person is experiencing from their perspective—that is, the capacity to place oneself in another's position, to put yourself in their shoes, as the saying goes. It is *feeling* with someone. I was asked in a session that I facilitated for the philanthropic arm of a large corporation if empathy was ever really possible if you had not experienced what another person had. Can you really walk in another's shoes if they are too small or too big for you? This is an important question.

The Winters Group 4E model suggests that empathy is possible only if you have gained exposure across differences, have had meaningful experiences with those who are different, and have engaged in ongoing education. These three Es lead to the fourth E: empathy. Even if you have not experienced what the other person has, you can, in learning more about their experiences, come closer to genuinely understanding what they may be feeling. In *We Can't Talk about That at Work,* I proposed the notion of reciprocal empathy—the ability to empathize with each other. We can get to this point of reciprocal empathy if we know what it is like to be the "other"—not necessarily in exact experiences but in relation to our emotional experiences.

For example, we sometimes have participants engage in an exercise called "Imagine How You'd Feel" to connect them to the emotions of being in the "other's" shoes. We have to do this on both sides of an issue. Can you understand why the person holds the viewpoint they do? Do you have an understanding of their cultural worldview? Have you asked them? What's at stake for them with this issue? What are they afraid of? What are they hoping for? Asking these questions can support you, if not in finding common ground, at least in finding some way to put yourself in their shoes—a step toward building trust.

Brené Brown, research professor at the University of Houston and renowned expert on empathy, offers that empathy and sympathy are very different.[2] She says that empathy is a skill that can bring people together and make people feel included, while sympathy creates an uneven power dynamic and can lead to more isolation and disconnection. Empathy builds connections—a required ingredient for trust and thus for inclusive conversations. Sympathy can lead to pity and unhelpful "at least" comments.

Sympathetic comments include:

> **Even worse.** This may sound like: "It could be much worse"…"Other people have gone through worse issues or more challenging situations."

  INTENT: Help someone see that what they're challenged with isn't "that bad."

  IMPACT: Invalidates experience, feelings.

> **Look on the bright side.** This may sound like: "At least you don't have to…"

  INTENT: Help someone focus on the positive, think optimistically.

  IMPACT: Undermines feelings or dismisses validity of the challenge or issue.

> **Problem solving.** This may sound like: "I can do this…" or "What do you need me to do?"

  INTENT: Make it better, help.

  IMPACT: Disconnects from emotion.

Empathetic statements sound more like this:

> **Acknowledge the situation.** "I am sorry that you are going through this," or "I see how that would be difficult."

> **Share how you feel.** "I don't know what to say," or "I can't imagine the impact on you."

> **Show gratitude that the person trusted you enough to share.** "Thank you for sharing with me," or "I am glad that you trusted me with this."

> **Show genuine interest and be supportive.** "Would you like to share more?" or "What I am hearing you say…(rephrase for clarity)?" or "What do you need right now?"

Learning to be more empathetic about the experiences of those who are different from you is critical in the trust-building process. Demonstrating that you care in your actions, even if you might not agree, is key for inclusive conversations.

CASE SITUATION
Demonstrating Empathy about the Impact of the Sociopolitical Climate

An African American male employee came to work distraught about a police-involved killing of an unarmed Black man. His supervisor, a white woman, saw that he was upset and asked what was wrong. He shared that he was angry and frustrated by yet another incident like this. His supervisor did not respond at all. She said nothing and walked away. A few months later, the Black male employee left the company. HR does not think this incident alone led to this high-potential employee taking another offer. However, it was thought to be a contributing factor. Offering grace to the supervisor, perhaps she just did not know what to say. Demonstrating empathy might have been what he needed to feel included, a sense of belonging, and the opportunity to build trust. She might have said: "I am sorry that you are going through this. I can't imagine how you feel. Thank you for sharing your feelings with me. Is there anything that I can do right now?"

I think sometimes when we are confronted with uncomfortable topics such as race, we may feel paralyzed and words will just not come. Or leaders might feel compelled to try to solve the issue. In this situation, perhaps the leader was caught off-guard, not sure why the Black employee was impacted. Developing skills for empathy are critical for anyone in a leadership position and for those who identify as allies.

Building Trust on a Team

Building trust is about building relationships. Cross-cultural work relationships are likely more difficult because of the fear of the unknown, perhaps disinterest in those who are different, and/or fear of saying something offensive. Therefore, it is harder to develop trust. Behavioral scientists say that leaders can build trust on teams with the following behaviors.

> **Frequent, honest communication—trust is built one interaction at a time.** If that frequent communication is not happening for certain people on the team, it follows that trust is not being developed. Studies have shown that honest communication is sometimes difficult across difference, especially conversations about race. In a 2016 *Fortune* study with interviews with African American men who were in leadership positions in their respective organizations, nearly

all had experienced conversations shutting down (or being shut out) when matters of race were brought up.[3] We must become comfortable talking about race.

> **Be impeccable with your word; do what you say you are going to do.** If the leader espouses to be an inclusion advocate, but their actions suggest otherwise (e.g., no visible diversity at the top; the same people selected for special assignments), there is a disconnect between the words and actions, which can erode trust.

> **Show people you care about them and their interests, as much as your own.** Demonstrate empathy. Get to know everyone on the team as an individual. This trust-building tenet also can be illusive for nondominant individuals in an organization. As pointed out in Chapter 3, women of color are less likely to get acknowledgment for contributions. Needless to say, this suggests there is work to do to create truly inclusive environments.

> **Speak from the heart.** Identify something good about the team member and emphasize this in your communication. Make sure that you include everyone when you pass out compliments and be careful that they are not stereotypical. For example, complimenting a person of color for being articulate is culturally offensive, as it suggests that it is unusual. In October 2019, as part of a social media campaign, the University of Missouri's Athletic Department tweeted pictures celebrating the diversity of their student athletes and staff. The intent behind the campaign was to showcase personal information about the students and why they are "more than a student athlete." The problem with the post

was the very different messaging chosen for Black athletes versus white athletes. The white athletes were characterized by career ambitions with statements such as "I am a future doctor" and "I am a future corporate financier." In stark contrast, the Black athletes' statements were more identity-focused like "I am an African American woman," "I am a brother," and "I value equality." I am sure that the developers thought they were saying something "good" about all of the athletes, but the biases were glaring. Mizzou issued an apology, took down the posts, and acknowledged that they took the statements from a video. In the video the full statement of sprinter Caulin Graves (an African American male) was, "I am a brother, uncle and best of all, I am a leader." Track athlete Arielle Mack (an African American woman) said, "I am an African-American woman, a sister, a daughter, and a future physical therapist." For some reason, only the first part of each statement was selected for the ad campaign.

› **Offer your willingness to listen.** Inclusive listening takes more skill. It means that you listen to yourself for your own biases, assumptions, and judgments.

› **Express your feelings with compassion and understanding.** Although this may be good general guidance, there are different cultural interpretations of the appropriate ways to share feelings. For example, women may be labeled as too emotionally expressive. By the same token, Blacks are often labeled as having too much "passion." Cultures that are less emotionally expressive may be viewed as lacking compassion. Therefore, we need to be mindful of how expressing feelings can be perceived coming from different identity groups.

> **Own your mistakes.** Honesty and integrity are crucial to building trusted teams. While owning your mistakes may sound good in theory, it may not work as well for subordinated groups in the workplace. Mistakes are magnified for historically marginalized groups. As mentioned in Chapter 4, a study by the National Bureau of Economic research showed that Blacks have to perform better than their white counterparts.[4] The study found that Black workers are more closely scrutinized, which increases the chances of errors and that they will be caught, and the result is that Black workers were more likely to be let go for "errors." This feeds into the well-entrenched belief that historically subordinated groups have to be "twice as good to get half as far." Therefore, owning mistakes can be riskier for historically underrepresented groups, thus impeding progress toward trust.

There is no quick fix to building trust across different dimensions of diversity. However, understanding the complex dynamics that make cross-cultural trust building more difficult is key for inclusive conversations.

SUMMARY

> Trust fosters our capacity for empathy, and conversely empathy recognizes that mistrust for many subordinated groups comes from historical injustices that have led to trauma that may be deeply embedded in the subconscious.

> If you are a member of the dominant group that has perpetrated the injustices, recognize that there may also be deep-seated internalized trauma that plays out as shock and denial.

> Authentic relationships build trust. Think about the real relationships that you have with your cultural others. What do you do to specifically build trust?

> Learn to be empathic. The capacity for empathy is key to building trusting relationships.

> If you are a leader, identify trust as a core value for the team. Allow the team to have input on what trust means to them and define specific trust-building behaviors.

> Don't expect to have real inclusive conversations if there has been no intentional attempt to build trust.

Discussion/Reflection Questions

1. How knowledgeable are you about historical reasons for cross-cultural mistrust? How can you/your team increase your understanding?

2. Do you think that enough trust exists in your organization to engage in inclusive conversations?

3. What impedes trust in your relationships? On your team? In your organization?

4. What is the relationship between trust and empathy?

5. What can you do to build your capacity for empathy?

-(NINE)-

Foster Belonging and Inclusion

> I matter and I am accepted unconditionally for who I am.

The diversity, equity, inclusion (DEI) world has recently added the idea of belonging to the lexicon as a necessary ingredient for inclusion. Companies like LinkedIn and MidPen Housing, an organization dedicated to developing affordable housing in the San Francisco Bay Area, are explicit in incorporating belonging in naming their efforts. For LinkedIn, it is DIB (diversity, inclusion, belonging), and MidPen named their effort ABIDE (advancing belonging, inclusion, diversity, equity). Belonging at work has been described as workers feeling secure, supported, accepted, and included. "Belonging" is what allows employees to feel like they can be their authentic selves without fear of different treatment or punishment. As discussed in Chapter 6, the absence fear is a vital condition for inclusive conversations.

As part of the research for this book, I conducted a nonscientific Internet survey and asked: What does belonging at work mean to you? These answers (see Table 9.1) represent a common theme from all respondents, consistent with what surfaced in the LinkedIn survey, summarized as a sense that "I matter and am accepted unconditionally for who I am."

Michael DeVaul, senior vice president and chief social responsibility officer for the Charlotte, North Carolina, YMCA, says that for him belonging is liberation. The YMCA's definition of belonging is the "shared experience of co-created unity that grounds identity and transforms 'otherness' into togetherness." According to research, belonging has a major impact on performance and retention. Based on the survey conducted by LinkedIn, shown in Figure 9.1, the top drivers of belonging are being recognized for one's accomplishments, having opportunities to express one's opinions freely (i.e., inclusive conversations), feeling that one's contributions in team meetings are valued, and feeling comfortable being oneself at work.[1]

None of these conditions are present in an environment of fear, or where trust does not exist, if there is not equity and an understanding of how power and privilege manifest in an organizational context (all conditions referenced in earlier chapters). The study showed that being recognized for accomplishments was more important to millennials than to **baby boomers** and more important for women than for men. Pat Waldros, LinkedIn's former chief human resources officer, says that "when we don't feel like we belong, we lose productivity because we waste time worrying about it and people of color spend 25–30% of their time worrying about how they fit in."[2] Worrying about fitting in falls into the fear categories of separation and ego-death discussed

---

TABLE 9.1 I Belong When...

I belong when:

"I am seen and see others who look like me. I belong when my perspective is valued."

"I am accepted for all of who I am without judgment or bias while also having access and opportunities for high-visibility projects."

"I am being valued and respected for who I am."

"I feel like I can bring my ideas, thoughts, and experiences without fear of what people will think about me when I share. I belong when my unique point of view is needed and valued."

"I feel like part of a community, respected and valued for similarities I share with others as well as differences I bring."

"I am supported, recognized, and appreciated for the work I do. I belong when I am seen as a full person with a life outside of work. I belong when I feel grace and understanding is extended when I need it."

"I am my full self and accepted as I am, not having to worry about covering any aspect of myself to create comfort for others."

"I feel comfortable—people listen to me and respect my opinion. I belong when I have friends, can be my real self, and am included in conversations, meetings, and social events."

"I feel like I am meant to be there and am able to feel confident in my reasons for being there. This confidence leads to being comfortable enough to share unique ideas but also express concerns when necessary."

"I can be fully transparent and accepted without judgment."

"I don't have to change who I am to be respected in a group."

"I feel safe and valued and respected in general by everyone, especially the person(s) to whom I directly report."

Source: The Winters Group, Inc.

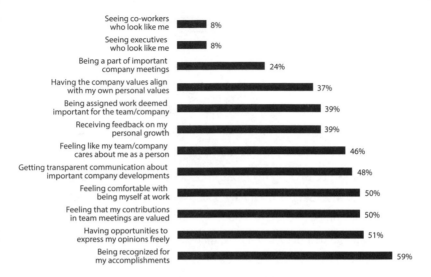

FIGURE 9.1 What Would Make You Feel Like You Belong at Work?
Source Based on LinkedIn Talent Blog by M. Huppert,
"Employees Share What Gives Them a Sense of Belonging at Work."

in Chapter 6. This worry can lead to loss of connectedness—not being wanted, respected, or valued—and can damage the ego by promulgating a loss of the sense of lovability, capability, and worthiness. As mentioned in Chapter 4, the research that women of color in particular do not feel that they are recognized for their contributions is a significant barrier to a sense of belonging.[3]

Fostering Belonging

Culture Amp, an HR-focused survey company, and the inclusion consultancy paradigm developed an inclusion survey for the tech industry to measure, among other things, belonging.[4] They found that belonging was a main determinant of inclusion regardless of gender, ethnicity, age group, or sexual orientation and that the correlation between belonging and engagement was markedly stronger for historically underrepresented groups. Among other recommendations, the Culture Amp Paradigm report recommended strengthening social bonds, building trusting relationships, and being intentional about inclusion.

Strengthening social bonds means that you are intentional about finding ways for people to get to know each other. As mentioned in Chapter 8, the Winters Group 4E model supports this recommendation. The 4 Es are exposure, experience, education, and empathy, which is not possible without the first three. We advocate for more exposure with those who are culturally different—to engage in different cultural experiences, to be educated about how different identity groups may have different worldviews based on different lived experiences. These experiences make empathy more plausible, as discussed in Chapter 8. Strengthening social bonds can happen in a variety of ways, for example:

> **Start every team meeting with a check-in.** At The Winters Group we use "share a personal and/or professional high for the week." Another question that we use to foster a sense of inclusion is "How are you entering this space today?"

> **Create intentional opportunities for the team to interface.** For example, The Winters Group orchestrated a wellness challenge, inviting everyone to set goals and share progress with the team. Those who exceed their self-established goals in the week are recognized.

> **Leverage technology.** We use Slack as a collaboration tool to allow for ongoing communication throughout the day. On

Fridays the team organically started to post humorous GIFs not videos to celebrate the upcoming weekend. Now it is almost like a competition to see who posts the funniest one.

The Winters Group is a 100 percent remote working environment, making it more difficult to strengthen social bonds, so we are very intentional in doing so. It is important to understand the different interests of employees and attempt to engage in social activities that are not directed more to one identity group. A golf outing may unintentionally exclude someone who has physical challenges or is just not interested in golf. While you cannot please everyone, incorporating a variety of activities will enhance a sense of belonging.

Trusting relationships is another recommendation of the Culture Amp Paradigm report. I explained the difficulties of developing trust across difference in Chapter 8. The study recommends developing mentoring relationships as a means of building trust. This is a good idea because mentorship has been shown to advance the careers of historically underrepresented groups. However, it is also documented that people of color, especially women of color, have difficulty finding mentors particularly as part of a formal program. I have heard several stories from women of color that the formal mentoring relationship may start out fine but over time both parties seems to lose interest and the sessions are canceled and rescheduled several times until they just fizzle out.

According to a study by the consulting firm Heidrick and Struggles, informal mentoring may be more effective. The study notes that only 9 percent of respondents found their mentor through a formal program.[5] According to the study, formal

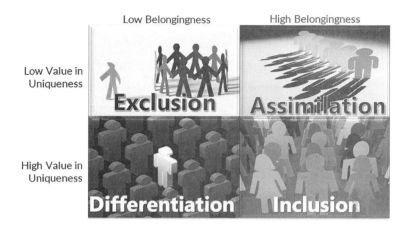

FIGURE 9.2 Belongingness
Source: Drawn by The Winters Group, Inc., based on content from
L. M. Shore et al., "Inclusion and Diversity in Work Groups."

mentoring programs had not cracked the code on how to create organic relationships. The key to great mentorship is that a bond of trust is formed, and the authors assert that an organic relationship where two individuals come together and want to invest time in that relationship will do just that.

Another recommendation for creating belonging from the Culture Amp Paradigm study is intentionality in developing an inclusive culture. Belonging is actually a component of inclusion, according to a study by L. M. Shore and colleagues.[6] They propose a model for inclusion as shown in Figure 9.2, where "uniqueness" and "belongingness" work together to create feelings of inclusion.[7] They postulate that uniqueness affords opportunities for improved group performance when the group values each person's uniqueness. When an individual is not accepted for their unique contributions, as supported by the LinkedIn study, the individual does not feel a sense of belonging.

For example, the widely documented phenomena that happens in meetings where a woman's idea might be ignored and later a man offers *essentially the same idea* and is lauded leads to women feeling excluded and ultimately to higher attrition rates. Research on women executives in top management teams suggests that, while women have a positive impact on firm performance, they leave their firms at a higher rate than male executives do.[8] The assimilation cell where there is high belongingness and low value in uniqueness reflects situations in which an individual who is unique is treated as an "insider" only if they are perceived as conforming with the dominant norms of culture. This is often referred to as "fit," which leads subordinated groups to sometimes feel they have to cover, code-shift, or minimize their differences.

The term **covering** was coined in 1963 by sociologist Erving Goffman to describe how even individuals with known **stigmatized identities** made a "great effort to keep the stigma from looming large."[9] Said another way, covering is the act of concealing something about yourself to avoid making other people feel uncomfortable or to lessen attention to a given characteristic. It's about downplaying pieces of your identity—such as race, religion, gender, disability, or sexual orientation—to avoid feelings of anxiety, frustration, or fear. Goffman gave the example of how President Franklin Delano Roosevelt ensured he was always seated behind a table before his Cabinet entered. President Roosevelt was not hiding his disability—everyone knew he was in a wheelchair. However, he was covering, making sure his disability was in the background of the interaction.

In 2006 legal scholar Kenji Yoshino further developed the concept of "covering."[10] He elaborated the four axes along which individuals can cover: appearance, affiliation, advocacy, and association. According to research, as many as 75 percent of people of color cover some aspect of their identity as well as 45 percent of white men. **Code-shifting** is the act of purposefully modifying your behavior in different settings to fit the dominant cultural norm. For example, you might not use vernacular that is considered ethnic or unique to your culture. "Minimization," a stage on the Intercultural Development Continuum, discussed in Chapter 3, might manifest for historically underrepresented groups as "going along to get along." Research shows that women have minimized their feminine features in favor of more traditional masculine traits to fit, and African American women may not wear a natural hairstyle in an attempt not to stand out. The assimilating behaviors may increase a sense of belongingness but at the same time diminish the sense of uniqueness. Emotional exhaustion can occur in this quadrant and lead to high turnover rates, especially when the "fitting" behaviors go against personal values.

When individuals experience low belongingness but are highly valued in the organization for their uniqueness, this is called differentiation. In some organizational settings, there may be individuals who offer unique and rare capabilities who are not considered or treated as organizational insiders. One way that organizations have put differentiation into practice is through free agency, whereby organizations purchase the services of highly talented and unique people to solve specific problems, and they remain as external consultants or contractors. Inclusion happens when an individual simultaneously experiences a high sense of belonging and a feeling that their uniqueness is valued. In this definition, belonging is a component of inclusion.

Fostering Belonging in K–12 Educational Settings

Based on a survey of educators conducted by the Education Week Research Center, a student's sense of belonging at school is important to academic achievement.[11] Even though most educators reported using strategies to help students feel welcome and safe at school, like greeting them at the classroom door each morning, many respondents reported that they "struggle" to help address some barriers to belonging. A full 41 percent of respondents reported that it is challenging or very challenging for them to address "the concerns of students who feel that they might be judged negatively based on their identity (e.g., disability status, gender, race/ethnicity)." A student who feels like the school environment is unjust or designed for someone from a different cultural background may become disengaged or not recognize his or her own potential, researchers say. That feeling can be reinforced by factors like a lack of diversity in school reading materials, unfair dress codes, or the sense that, for example, a mostly white, female teaching staff relates to some students differently than others.

The Winters Group has supported the CMS (Charlotte-Mecklenburg School) district in Charlotte, North Carolina, for several years in improving the cultural proficiency of its eighteen thousand employees, from the superintendent to those who provide transportation. The vison for CMS, which is stressed in many ways throughout the district, including all of the training sessions and their literature, is "every child, parent, caregiver, visitor and fellow employee, feels welcomed, expected, valued, and appreciated every day." District bus drivers are included in the training to explore with them what this vision means in their role and their responsibility in ensuring that every child feels welcomed and expected. A key to belonging is feeling that you are "expected."

Valda Valbrun, CEO of the Valbrun Consulting Group and K–12 principal strategist with The Winters Group, supported the district in developing the vision and said that there was a lot of conversation about the words "welcomed" and "expected" as to whether they were redundant. Valbrun lobbied to keep both words because there is an important distinction. You can be welcoming, but when you are expecting someone to come, you may do something special just for that person. Both terms together create a sense of belonging. Educators can engage in the following to enhance a sense of belonging for all students, especially the most vulnerable:

> Increase cultural competence by learning more about the cultural framework and norms of your students. If you don't know about behaviors that might be cultural, you can misinterpret to the detriment of the student. For example, a Black child who talks out in class without raising their hand, even after many admonitions by the teacher, might be labeled as disruptive. However, maybe their faith expression is one known as call-and-response, a discourse pattern associated with African American religious tradition. The child may be learning at church that you just talk back and forth. The interpretation of disruption would lead to some type of punishment, whereas considering the possibility that it is cultural would lead to different actions. The behavior might still need to be adjusted, but the approach would be very different.

> Show a genuine interest in each child by learning what they like and don't like.

> Learn to pronounce a student's name.

Do not schedule tests or project due dates on religious holidays.

Engage and validate the social identity of all students during class.

Do not anticipate a student's emotional responses based on gender, sexual orientation, race, or ethnicity.

Refrain from using the term "illegals" to reference undocumented students.

Do not deny the experiences of students by questioning the credibility and validity of their stories.

Avoid expecting students of any particular group to "represent" the perspectives of others of their race, gender, or other dimension of difference in class discussions or debates.

Ask students about what makes them feel like they belong. Let them tell you in their own words what it looks like and feels like for them.

Recognize that dress codes can foster a sense of belonging or not. Find ways to embrace the uniqueness of each child and be creative with dress codes to the extent possible.

Do not assume the gender of any student.

Avoid assigning projects that ignore differences in socioeconomic status and inadvertently penalize students with fewer financial resources.

Do not exclude students from accessing student activities due to high financial costs.

Avoid assuming that students of particular ethnicities must speak another language or must not speak English.

Refrain from complimenting students of color on their use of "good" English.

Do not ask students with hidden disabilities to identify themselves in class.

Pay attention and correct student-to-student inequitable behavior.

Emphasize the child's assets rather than deficiencies.

Develop lesson plans that focus on the cultural heritage of the students.

Ensure that the books you choose include the identities of your students. They need to see themselves in the teaching so that they feel that they matter.

Develop mutually respectful relationships with parents and guardians. Let them know that they matter. Accept them for who they are, treating them always with dignity. Empathize with their unique situations and be flexible in how, when, and where you will meet or talk.

Hold equitable conversations with parents and guardians considering the power dynamics that might be present as discussed in Chapter 5.

Often, when considering the lower socioeconomic levels of many students in large public school systems, the focus is on what they don't have rather than their strengths. Children easily pick up on the biases that teachers might unintentionally perpetuate. My daughter-in-law, Dr. Kamilah Legette, a research associate at University of North Carolina at Chapel Hill, studies the impact of bias on students of color. Her research revealed that children know when their teachers perceive them to be at some type of deficit.[12] Children answered her queries with comments like:

> I mean just because they think they can just look at you and say "Oh, you're a bad child," but they actually don't even know you, so that's just what they think before they actually get to know you, but then when they get to know you, their opinions would

change and they would think, and then they'll know that you're nice, you're not a bad child.

They didn't really think that I had the answer. I was raising my hand to say something, but like the teachers kept calling on white people, not me. But I keep trying. It can be kinda hard, because I feel like my teachers don't like me or think I know things.

It's just, I can't really explain it to you, but sometimes it's like I can tell at first they think I'm going to be a certain way and then they find out I'm different.

Cultivating a sense of inclusion in the workplace, school, and other organizational settings requires intentional, ongoing actions. Those who feel excluded or compelled to fit narrow cultural norms will not thrive and will likely not be willing to engage in inclusive conversations.

SUMMARY

- › Feeling like you belong is a basic human need for children and adults alike.

- › Belonging is a component of inclusion.

- › A feeling of inclusion is a core condition for inclusive conversations.

- › Organizations should be intentional in understanding what inclusion is in their organizational context and how to achieve it by conducting ongoing pulse checks. The results of research can serve as conversation starters.

- › A sense of belonging is very individual, contextual, and even situational. While there is a mutual responsibility for achieving it, power dynamics (as discussed in Chapter 5) can have a huge impact on the outcome. Therefore, those in power positions have a greater responsibility for ensuring that a culture of inclusion is actualized.

Discussion/Reflection Questions

1. What is inclusion? What is belonging? How do they work together? Develop a list of behaviors that foster inclusion and belonging.

2. What intentional activities can you engage in to foster a sense of belonging?

3. In what ways does your organizational culture encourage assimilation? How can you begin to dismantle that norm for one who values the uniqueness of each individual?

4. What are some examples of the need to code-shift, cover, or minimize in your organizational culture?

5. How does assimilation impact performance?

─{ TEN }─

Acknowledge and Own Whiteness

> Whiteness, like Blackness, is a reality. However, whiteness is invisible to many white people and painfully visible and impactful for many Black people. If we don't talk about whiteness, we cannot have inclusive conversations.

In a recent training session with a faith-based group, a female pastor shared as part of the debrief of a self-awareness identity exercise that she never thinks about her race. One of the African American participants retorted that he *always* thinks about his race. It was a defining moment in the session. The white woman went on to say that she tries not to notice race—that she wants to bring neutrality to the dialogue and race doesn't matter to her. The African American participant responded that race *always* matters and invited her to not only notice it but to learn more about racial dynamics. In another session, participants were asked to name four aspects of their identity that are most important to them. A white woman said: "Five years ago I would not have included 'privileged white woman' as important to my identity. I am learning how my whiteness shapes how I see the world and that I am a part of a system, even if I don't like it or intentionally perpetuate it, that keeps whites in the dominant position." She went on to share that she grew up in a white, liberal environment and thought that because she harbored no racist views, that was enough. She in essence defined race as something Blacks had, not her—she unconsciously perceived herself as "raceless."

These two examples summarize the issue: white people, by and large, do not see themselves as a part of a race. One of the reasons we are stuck and not making more progress in inclusion is the oblivion on the part of too many white people of how their whiteness is pervasive, dominant, and impedes progress toward inclusion, equity, and belonging. This is not about denigrating white people. It is about acknowledging the basic ontology of a deeply embedded system that normalizes white people. We can talk about whiteness only in the context of Blackness and vice versa. If race did not exist, there would be nothing to discuss, no comparisons to make. It is this racial binary that is at the crux of how all of US society is structured. Let's face it, the history of race in the US context is really about Blacks and whites. Acknowledging that "white" is a social construct with its own ontology is critical for meaningful, inclusive conversations.

Other countries have had their own history with racial dynamics that have played out differently based on their politics, economics, and attitudes toward race. For the purposes of this chapter, I focus on US racial dynamics. The very notion of "whiteness" can be so controversial for some white people that they might reject the idea before giving it due consideration. Whiteness is not negative. It just is. Actually, the paradox is that white people created the racial hierarchy, and many now deny that it exists. We have to get comfortable talking about race to have inclusive conversations.

A Brief History of Race and Racism in the United States

People have not always been classified by skin color. As a matter of fact, scientists assert that race is a social construct with little biological distinction. The word "race" first appeared in the English language in 1508 in a poem by William Dunbar referring to a line of kings.[1] Throughout much of human history, societies have enslaved others, often as a result of conquest or war, even debt, but not because of physical characteristics or a belief in natural inferiority. Due to a unique set of historical circumstances, the United States was the first system where all the enslaved people eventually shared similar physical characteristics.

However, that was not always the case. In the early years of the American colony, many Africans and poor whites worked side-by-side as indentured servants. Black and white men who broke their servant contract were equally punished. As indentured servants both Blacks and whites were allowed to buy their freedom. Historically, the English enslaved only non-Christians, and not, in particular, Africans. An enslaved person could become free by converting to Christianity. This meant that the indentured servant workforce was not permanent, and as it started to dwindle, the landowners had to find another way to ensure a stable workforce for the plantations. Thereafter they decided to use a status that was not changeable—skin color. Enslaved people, especially those who could be identified by skin color, could not move on and compete with the slave owners as white indentured servants could. Thus, the system of racial slavery was institutionalized around 1676.

To continue to justify enslaving Blacks throughout the centuries, theories of "scientific racism" became widespread and generally accepted. Numerous books and articles were written during the four-hundred-year period of slavery that Blacks were biologically inferior, possessing lower IQs, and closer to monkeys than other humans. Vestiges of theories of Black inferiority based on "scientific proof" haunt us today. Consider the previously mentioned cancellation of Rosanne Barr's sitcom after she used an ape analogy in a tweet about Valerie Jarrett, an African American presidential adviser. This act led to the cancellation of her television sitcom. Or the white supremacist Dylann Roof, who in 2015 went into an African American church in Charleston, South Carolina, and killed nine Black worshippers. In the crude manifesto he posted on the Internet in 2015, he wrote: "Negroes have lower IQ's, lower impulse control, and higher testosterone levels in general. These three things alone are a recipe for violent behavior."[2]

Whites Are "Raceless"?

Even with the long and distasteful history in the United States of race and **racism**, a classification manufactured by whites, many sociologists assert that US whites think that they are in essence "raceless" or "cultureless." Race is diversity's four-letter word. Consciously for some and unconsciously for many more, race is not a "nice" thing to talk about. Some white people are so averse to any discussion of race, that objections are swift and direct any time the topic surfaces, with comments like: "Diversity is about more than race" and "Oh, no, not the race card again."

These kinds of statements, which are not uncommon, are sure to squash any hope of having inclusive conversations. Perhaps the disdain for conversations about race emanates from historical guilt and shame that is etched in the intergenerational DNA of some white people. For others, the aversion might come from a belief that race is not important.

In a 2019 Pew survey on race in America, Blacks were more likely than Hispanics or Asians, and much more likely than whites, to say that their race is central to their identity.[3] A full 75 percent of Black adults responded that being Black is extremely or very important to how they think of themselves, versus just 15 percent of whites who responded that being white is very or extremely important to their identity. As such, white people typically do not name their race as a part of their core identity in The Winters Group training sessions and sometimes seem annoyed or visibly uncomfortable when Blacks do. Whites more often answer the exercise that invites them to share core aspects of their identity with "human," "caring person," "free spirit," or "mother," while Blacks are more apt to name Black or African American or Afro-Caribbean.

Understanding Whiteness Theory

Increasingly there is discourse about whiteness and the need to pay more attention to the concept of whiteness. In studies of race, we most often focus on the "racialized" other. In college curricula race courses focus on the victims of racism as the primary content. It is only in the past thirty years or so that whiteness as a discipline to study has gained popularity. **Whiteness theory** examines how whiteness is normalized in culture, creating an unawareness to the set of privileges associated with white identity, also known as white privilege. Whiteness theory posits that whiteness is the default of American culture, and as a result of this default, white people cannot see the advantages and disadvantages of being white due to a lack of "cultural subjectiveness" toward whiteness.[4]

Inasmuch as the idea that whiteness is normalized, it may make it invisible to those who are white. It is like the fish-in-water analogy: the fish is unaware that it is in water until you take it out. Therefore, it is not surprising that when we ask participants in learning experiences to think about aspects of their identity, for whites their race does not often emerge. One of the first notions of whiteness came from feminist and antiracist activist Peggy McIntosh's classic work that white Americans have little racial awareness of or consciousness about themselves.[5] Her paper "White Privilege: Unpacking the Invisible Knapsack" is considered groundbreaking and seminal.

The author of *Good White People*, Shannon Sullivan, Chair and Professor of Philosophy at the University of North Carolina at Charlotte, asserts that well-meaning white liberals embrace an attitude of "goodness" and as such are insulted by any notion that they contribute to racial disparities. But this serves to shut down authentic conversation about race.[6] White liberals believe their individual good intentions are enough, which results in less concern for systemic racism and privilege. Sullivan says that white people have four basic strategies to establish their lack of racism, including blaming lower-class whites for continuing to perpetuate racism; demonizing slaveholders; emphasizing their color blindness; as well as their attitudes of shame and guilt. She calls these "distancing strategies" and recommends a "new ethos" that moves to activism and **agency** for racial justice rather than "self-righteous" distancing from it. Sullivan encourages white people to acknowledge their whiteness rather than disown it or pretend it doesn't exist.

Celebrating Whiteness

Travis Jones, principal strategist for The Winters Group, wrote for our blog *The Inclusion Solution* about the "power of whiteness."[7] He recounted an event where comedian W. Kamau Bell challenged a white audience to start owning and naming positive aspects of white culture. His approach and appeal is awkward for white audience members, even more evidence of how uncommon talking about white culture is for many people. Bell has Black audience members lift their fists in unison and chant "black power" as a sign of solidarity—the response is almost unanimous. Immediately after he asks white people to do the same, this time chanting "white power"—the response is silence, unease, and awkward laughter. Bell follows up with the point that if white people don't start owning and celebrating the positive aspects of white culture, they leave the door open for white supremacists, racist politicians, or race deniers to be the only voices speaking on behalf of white people.

In a recent session with a group of ten diversity practitioners from a major company who represented different identity groups, the white participants agreed that talking about their "whiteness" is extremely uncomfortable because they feel a sense of guilt and shame about the connotations of that identity. However, the group concurred that society needs to have discussions about whiteness as an identity to advance diversity, equity, and inclusion in society. They agreed that their organization was not at all ready for such discussions. I conjecture that DEI professionals in most organizations would share that sentiment. Part of society's growing edge is acknowledging and learning how to discuss whiteness.

In his *Inclusion Solution* post, Travis invited readers to join him in thinking about "positive" forms of white culture. He stressed that it should go without saying that this question does not imply that there is inherently anything negative about white people or that there aren't countless positive aspects of culture that white people predominantly enjoy. But the question is important because he posited that white people don't typically describe these cultural elements as tied to whiteness—choosing instead cultural markers other than race. In fact, "color-blindness" is one of the markers of whiteness itself—as a dominant culture—that makes it difficult to describe or pin down white cultural attributes.

Some readers might be thinking, "But how can you describe white culture?" No culture has a definitive set of characteristics, and whiteness has the added anomaly of "invisibility" that works to evade attempts at identifying patterns. One aspect of white culture *is* the unspoken assumption that white is the norm and every other group is the "other." Another major characteristic of white culture is that it is Eurocentric, a worldview centered on or biased toward Western civilization. This is evident in how history is recorded and told, and which civilizations are touted (perhaps subtly or not so subtly) as superior. As an example, schoolchildren are taught that Christopher Columbus "discovered" America. The problem with this assertion is that Native people already occupied what is known as America. Western white culture is characterized by individualism, preference for the written word over oral traditions, direct communication styles, concentrated power, and aversion to conflict. Notwithstanding some of the negative aspects such as colonialism and imperialism, on a more positive side, white culture can be attributed with many advances in the arts and sciences and supporting world allies in the quest for peace and human rights.

Obviously, there is "good" and "bad" in every culture, and it is important to build a narrative that recognizes "white" as a distinct culture with its positives and negatives just like any other culture. Currently white supremacists are defining what it means to be white—hate mongering, violent separatists who would annihilate any group that is not white.

Distinguishing "Racist" from "Racism"

Robin DiAngelo's book *What Does It Mean to Be White?* advances the idea that most white people abhor being labeled racists.[8] Of course, no one wants to be called racist, but DiAngelo says that liberal white people understand racism as an interpersonal evil and ignore that it is really a system requiring collective attention (see Chapter 1). They confuse "racist" with "racism." Being associated with racism in any way conjures up defensiveness that DiAngelo calls "white fragility" (described in Chapter 6) and may lead to "whitesplaining," where a white person explains to Black people the true nature of racism from their worldview, obviously lacking lived experience as a Black person. We also must consider that the "racist = bad; not racist = good" binary ignores all the evidence from brain science that we internalize racist messages from a racist society that becomes a part of who we are—whether we're aware of it or believe it. It does not make us inherently "bad."

Whiteness and Inclusive Conversations

What are some considerations about whiteness in inclusive conversations?

> **Acknowledge whiteness.** In diversity training sessions where you are asked about identity, do not ignore your race. We need to increase the 15 percent of white people who perceive their race as a part of their identity. Inclusive conversations about race are impossible with a color-blind worldview. In a recent session, we did an exercise asking participants to share their core identities. I first offered mine as an example and included African American. One of the white male participants shared, "You have a significant identity as an African American. I hesitated to put 'white male' because it doesn't mean anything." Everyone's racial identity is meaningful.

> **Whether you think so or not, race is a dynamic in all cross-race conversations.** That is not to say that I am necessarily recommending that you explicitly state it, but if you are white, be aware of it; the Black person certainly is, even if they would not admit it. If you are white, ask yourself: "What dynamic does my whiteness play in this conversation? How do I **decenter the dominant narrative?**" Depending on the extent of the presence of the conditions that I laid out in Chapter 2, it might be safe to name the race dynamic. For the Black person in the dialogue, ask yourself: "To what extent do I think this person is **woke** and is aware of their whiteness? Am I able/willing to give grace and forgiveness? Can I exercise my power/agency in this conversation?"

> **Create equity in the conversation.** Use the suggestions in Chapter 5.

> **Commit to take action.** Try to get past the shame, blame, denial, fear, and other emotions that a white person may harbor in a society that is founded on racist principles. As I recommend in Chapter 1, own your responsibility as a part of the collective guilt to be committed to take action. As the Black person in the conversation, be mindful of the power dynamics and defensiveness on the part of the white person. Handle it by asking clarifying questions like this: "That is interesting, what makes you think that?" Use opportunities to educate as appropriate and even use the oops, ouch, and educate model outlined in Chapter 7.

> **Acknowledging whiteness includes calling out white people.** In a post penned by Adam Mansbach and W. Kamau Bell in *Salon*, the authors recommend that acknowledging whiteness includes calling out white people as people of color call out their own when needed.[9] For example, Blacks on social media have objected to comments by Dr. Ben Carson (former neurosurgeon and current US Secretary of Housing and Urban Development) when they do not represent the sentiments of many Black people. Bell believes that white people should do the same with Donald Trump. "As a white person, I am appalled at what the president said about X," for example. This of course is difficult if whiteness as a culture is invisible to white people. Bell says, "It's a way to claim and use whiteness, to wield it with authority rather than apology,

and that's something white anti-racists seldom get the chance to do."

> **Refrain from whitesplaining.** This is explained in more detail in Chapter 11. It is normal for someone from the dominant group to unconsciously believe that they are entitled to comment on all matters or at least have a viewpoint that is valid because of their assumed position as the norm. Rather than *tell* Black people, ask.

Travis concludes his *Inclusion Solution* post with the belief that you have to focus on self-awareness by acknowledging whiteness. This starts "with a very serious and honest self-reflective look inside ourselves—at the messages, images, values, beliefs, and experiences we've 'soaked up' living in a culture that continues to produce racial inequity and injustice. Maybe we don't fully get to the bottom of whiteness; but this is where we start."[10]

─────────────── **SUMMARY** ───────────────

> Acknowledging whiteness is critical for inclusive conversations.

> Many white people see themselves as "raceless" due to their position as the "dominant culture."

> Conversations about race are very uncomfortable for many whites, leading to defensiveness and denial.

> Learn the history of race and racism.

> Acknowledging whiteness can promote a positive narrative to counteract the perspectives of white supremacist groups.

Discussion/Reflection Questions

1. How can discussions of "whiteness" enhance inclusion efforts?

2. Why does it inhibit inclusive conversations not to acknowledge whiteness?

3. Why is it so difficult to discuss race and whiteness?

4. Discuss the history of race from your cultural context and how those vestiges of history continue to play out today.

5. Discuss the difference between "racist" and "racism."

ELEVEN

Mind Your Words

> Words matter. Words can hurt. Words can do irreparable damage. Or words can encourage. Words can affirm. Words can include and foster equity, empathy, and belonging.

We vividly remember the words that hurt, that cut at our very sense of self-worth long after they have been spoken. When I worked in the corporate world in the 1970s, I wore my hair in a short Afro style. One day, a colleague came into my office unannounced and uninvited and very directly asked: "Will your hair grow?" I answered in the affirmative and his response was "You ought to let it." I was flabbergasted that he had the audacity to say something so insulting to me. I was so self-conscious after that encounter that I thought about buying a wig or straightening my hair. It impacted my ability to concentrate on my work, and I certainly did not feel included. Even though this happened in the late 1970s, women of color still receive messages today, whether direct or indirect, that natural hair is not appropriate for the workplace. It erodes our self-concept and well-being. These messages take all that we have to muster up resilience and grace and forgiveness.

Microaggressions

My experience is an example of a **microaggression**—brief, sometimes subtle, everyday comments that either consciously or unconsciously disparage others based on their personal characteristics or perceived group membership.[1] Microaggressions exclude, demean, and create inequitable work, school, and broader societal environments. The term "microaggression" was first coined in 1978 by scholar Chester M. Pierce to describe a phenomenon of subtle negative exchanges directed toward African Americans.[2] There is also a related term, **"microinequities,"** which is often used interchangeably with microaggressions. I prefer the term "microaggressions" for its specificity in categorizing difference and sometimes the intentional slights.

The concept of **microaffirmations**, advanced by Mary Rowe when she was MIT ombudsman, is the antidote to microinequities and microaggressions. These are small but meaningful positive comments that create a sense of belonging and value. Even the seemingly innocuous comments like "nice job" or "I really value your input" or " I appreciated your role in making the project a success" can make a tremendous difference for employees. Likewise, microaffirmations for children can positively impact their academic performance as pointed out in Chapter 9. Things like pronouncing a student's name correctly, giving praise for improvements and correct answers make a real difference.

Scholars have proposed three categories of microaggressions that can occur in everyday interactions: **microassaults, microinsults,** and **microinvalidations.** The category for a particular microaggression usually depends on the intent as well as the impact the language has on those who hear it. Microaggressions might be related to race, gender, sexual orientation, socioeconomic status, religion, or other aspects of one's social identity. Most often microaggressions are verbal slights in words that are spoken, although they may also be nonverbal.[3] The list below provides examples of the three different types of microaggressions and how they might play out in everyday encounters.

Microassaults

These are conscious, deliberate, and either subtle or explicit biased attitudes, beliefs, or behaviors that are communicated to marginalized groups through verbalizations or behaviors. Examples include:

> "You women are too emotional to negotiate with our top suppliers."

> "Black parents don't care about their children's education."

> "You are going to need to lose that accent if you want to move up here. People can't understand you."

> "Those poor people just aren't smart enough to pull themselves out of poverty."

> Said to a person in a wheelchair: "I know it will be hard for you to keep up at our retreat because we will be doing a lot of physical activity."

> Banning certain hairstyles like locks.

> Said to a Black person (recall stereotypes about Black people and fried chicken): "I ordered fried chicken for lunch because I thought you would enjoy it."

> "White people have made more contributions to society than any other group."

> Jokes aimed at a particular identity group in the name of innocent "fun."

Microinsults

These are interpersonal communications that convey stereotypes, rudeness, and insensitivity that demean a person's identity. Unlike microassaults, microinsults are often committed unconsciously and may seem more subtle. Examples include:

> Said to someone who does not look white or who speaks with another accent: "Where are you from?" Answer: "The United States." "No, really, where are you from?"

> **Cultural misappropriation.** This is behaving or acting in ways that represent a culture you are not a part of and interpreted as demeaning by that culture such as white, non-Sikh models wearing turbans. For Sikhs, turbans are not fashion objects; rather, they are highly significant to their religion.

> Said to a woman of color with natural hair: "Can I touch your hair?"

> "You gays are so creative—such an asset to the team."

> Said to a Black person, as if it is unusual: "You are so articulate."

> Constant mispronunciation of names.

> "You Asians are so good at math."

> "I don't see your color."

> "You people" (referring to a historically marginalized group, which has a derogatory, polarizing tone).

> Said to a Muslim woman with a hijab or a Sikh with a turban: "We don't allow any employee to wear a 'hat.'"

Microinvalidations

These are communication cues that exclude, negate, or nullify the thoughts, feelings, or experiential realities of certain groups. Examples include:

> **Gaslighting.** This refers to psychological manipulation toward a historically marginalized group to make the receiver feel that the situation is their fault. "Women put themselves in a position for sexual harassment. They are just as responsible."

> "Why do you people always call the race card?"

> "It is no big deal. Why are you so sensitive?" (It is obviously a big deal for the person. Listen and practice empathy.)

> "Don't say, Black lives matter. All lives matter."

> Ignoring a woman's input in a meeting and praising a man for the same idea.

> **Mansplaining.** This occurs when a cisgender man condescendingly explains something to a woman in a manner that suggests she can't possibly know what he's

talking about or what she is talking about, even though she has expertise on the topic. He is the real authority (exhibiting dominant group power and privileged behavior—i.e., men know best).

> **Whitesplaining.** When someone from a dominant group explains to audiences of color the true nature of racism. Said by a white person: "In general, racism is a thing of the past. I don't think it is an issue at our organization."

> **Tone policing.** "If you did not say it so expressively (e.g., angrily, loudly, passionately), I might have been able to hear it."

> Not including certain people in meeting invites.

> Speaking in binaries, using "either/or" or "but" (negative) language rather than "both/and" (additive) language.

> **Distancing language.** This refers to statements that people may use when trying to assure others that they are on the "right side" of the issues. Examples are: "Some of my friends are Black," or "I don't see why this is so hard," or a white person saying, "I get it and don't know why others don't." They are distancing themselves from those whites who "don't get it."

Addressing Microaggressions

Microassaults are usually intentional. How you address them depends on the situation and the relationship with the individual. Who is this individual to me? What is the relationship? If there is no relationship, and will not likely ever be one, you might want to ignore it and chock it up to their ignorance. You use emotional energy every time you have to respond to a microaggression. If after exploring, you decide that even though you have no relationship with the person, it is worth saying something, keep it brief and factual.

The comment on my hairstyle that I encountered in the 1970s is an example of a microassault. I did not handle it well. I literally was speechless and did not provide any response. However, in a brave space environment here is what I might have said:

MICROASSUALT: Will your hair grow? You ought to let it.

ANSWER: What I am hearing is that you like long hair. I prefer short hair. Perhaps you did not intend to insult me, but that was clearly the impact. Your preferred hairstyle has nothing to do with my work or our peer relationship.

Ideally, my colleague would self-reflect, apologize, and learn from his mistake. However, if the microassualt is intentional, that may not necessarily be the outcome. You may decide that you should discontinue any relationship with this person. If it is a co-worker, you have to think about the option of reporting microassaults to management, the risk versus the reward, the culture of the organization, and a host of other matters. I chose not to report the microassault and I suffered the pain that it caused for a long time as forgiveness was not even something I considered. I was not aware of the psychological freedom that it might have afforded me.

Microinsults

These are difficult to address because they are often subtle. In Chapter 3 I addressed how to handle the microinsult of "I don't see color."

MICROINSULT: May I touch your hair? (Asked of an African American woman)

ANSWER: I would not be comfortable with that. May I ask why you would want to? Are there questions that I can answer for you about my hair?

INSULTER: It is just different and I have never seen a style like this.

ANSWER: Thank you for your curiosity. However, I don't think it is appropriate to touch my hair or any other part of my body. Has anyone asked you if they could touch your hair? It makes me feel as if I am an aberration and not normal. Different in a strange way.

INSULTER: Thank you. I did not mean to insult you but obviously I have. As part of my learning about differences, I would like to hear more about African-inspired styles.

ANSWER (THERE IS A CHOICE HERE): If you do not feel comfortable "teaching," politely decline. You might also suggest the co-worker do their own research.

Microinvalidations

These probably hurt the most because they erode self-esteem and often make you question your capability, which can lead to internalized oppression (discussed in Chapter 3). Gaslighting is particularly damaging if it is a repetitive experience. This is where your self-concept will be tested. You might ask, "Is there something wrong with me?" Gaslighting can also put you in a defensive mode if you find yourself continually responding to it. Recognize it, engage in self-affirmations, and respond in ways that serve to put an end to the behavior. Here's an example:

YOUR CO-WORKER: It is your fault that this project is off schedule. You took so much time off when your baby was ill.

YOU: You know that I had nothing to do with the schedule. There were a number of issues including materials coming late from the supplier.

YOUR CO-WORKER: I don't accept that.

YOU: There are many reasons that we are off schedule, and I am not one of them.

Whitesplaining and Mansplaining

Whitesplaining and **mansplaining** are really demeaning for the receiver. I think sometimes men engage in mansplaining because they are known to be "fixers" (women want them to listen and they want to fix the situation), and with whitesplaining there may be unconscious bias that Blacks are less intelligent or that in white people's dominant racial position they are entitled to be experts in racial matters as well.

Here's a good response to "splaining": "Thank you, and there is a lot more that I could add to that from my expertise/lived experience." If the "splaining" is actually not accurate—I would be interested in knowing where the information comes from. You might say: "I have information that would not support your assertions here." Depending on the setting—one-on-one, team, and the audience, peers or superiors—you may need to decide when to correct erroneous information, at the time or later in private.

Advice to "'splainers": Be self-aware of your tendency to "'splain" and engage in metacognitive behavior (described in Chapter 3) to explore why you feel compelled to explain. Know your power position. If you are white, be careful not to try and be an expert on race, unless you really are.

Ignoring Women's Input

Women need men as allies to recognize that this is a widespread phenomenon. A woman offers an idea in the workplace, and it is ignored until soon after a man recommends essentially the same thing.

One solution: Stay attentive to whose ideas are validated and whose are not. Make sure that you acknowledge everyone's input even if you don't agree. Validation can be as simple as saying, "Thank you for that idea." If a man's idea is validated after a woman has offered a similar one already, try this: "Thank you for confirming the idea that Amy offered a few moments ago." This is an example of effective allyship.

Tone Policing

This is a way of invalidating concerns because of the the tone in which the message was delivered. **Tone policing** dismisses the "issue" (e.g., the inequity, injustice, oppression, and the impact it has) and centers on the way in which the issue was communicated (e.g., "you sounded angry or divisive"). Some have defended tone policing as a way to challenge how advocates for justice "play on emotion" without reason or evidence. For example, in advocacy or social justice spaces as well as in the media, tone policing might sound like:

NATIVE AMERICAN/INDIGENOUS LEADER SHARING: Our government has turned its back on our community! Our government and policies are racist and have impacted, even taken, the lives of thousands in our community. We want action!

ANALYST ON MEDIA OUTLET: The reality is, more would probably get done if they focused on being civil in communicating their issues. You can't call the government racist and expect a response that is favorable to your efforts.

We should learn to listen to the concerns and issues regardless of how they are delivered. Ask yourself: "Why is this delivery method so difficult for me? It is not my preferred style? I think it is disingenuous. Why do I think that?" Try to focus on the message and why the anger and frustration might be a part of the message.

Distancing Language

Distancing language negates, simplifies, or recommends delaying action. It stalls progress in a conversation by continuing to ask for better, clearer, or different definitions of the problem. Here are a few distancing techniques that inhibit inclusive conversations.[4]

Definitions game. Requests for clear, absolute definitions of terms around race, -isms, culture, and so on usually lead to involved discussion and no consensus on definitions. This can serve to avoid discussions of the real issues. We continue to play the definitions game and also the "add new words to the DEI lexicon." Part of the reason for adding new words is that old ones become stigmatized. For example, the term "diversity," once primarily positive, now conjures up negative connotations. Some see it as a code word for affirmative action, or preferential treatment for historically underrepresented groups. As mentioned in Chapter 10, some white men do not see their issues included under the diversity definition. When engaging in inclusive conversations, it is important to come to common ground on definitions.

It is also important not to continue to add new terms that confuse more than clarify DEI work. For example, in Chapter 9 I outlined a condition of creating a sense of belonging in order to have inclusive conversations. "Belonging" has been defined by researchers as a component of inclusion and perhaps does not need its own separate category, which is why I combined the two concepts. Many have a difficult time defining "belonging" as distinct from "inclusion" as my survey in Chapter 9. Some organizations also include **accessibility** in their acronym, using DEAI (diversity, equity, accessibility, inclusion). I think that "accessibility" is embedded in the definition of equity. The American Alliance of Museums defines accessibility as "giving equitable access to everyone along the continuum of human ability and experience. Accessibility encompasses the broader meanings of compliance and refers to how organizations make space for the characteristics that each person brings."[5] Also as mentioned in Chapter 9, some organizations choose the acronym DIB (diversity, inclusion, belonging), while others use ABIDE (advancing, belonging, inclusion, diversity, equity).

In our quest to be inclusive of all of the possible ways that we might exclude, we continually add to the lexicon. We may do this to highlight the complexities of this work in digestible more simplistic ways. Unfortunately, I think the more we add to DEI vocabulary, the more we confuse. This makes discussions about our work even more difficult.

> **Instant solutions.** This leads to oversimplification by choosing and pushing single solutions to racism or other forms of oppression. It could be a type of avoidance. If sincere, it is unproductive because there are no simple solutions. Clients often ask The Winters Group to offer a simple solution to resolve DEI issues without considering the systemic root causes. Inclusive conversations need to acknowledge that there are no easy answers and seek to get to the root rather than just the symptoms.

> **You've come a long way.** This focuses on what changes have or may have occurred since people of color and other marginalized communities began the struggle for civil rights. Perhaps the message is that people of color should be satisfied with the progress. I believe that we should acknowledge the advances, yet it is important not to discount what still needs to be done.

> **"After I…"** This attitude leads to focusing on all of the things that prevent us from acting right now to challenge "isms." It sounds like "It will be done when…(some magic occurrence)." Be aware of the words that you use that might serve to maintain the status quo and distance you from the issue.

> **"You are being too sensitive."** I referenced a situation in the introduction where a participant in a session asked if we can be too sensitive and too politically correct. Someone

had objected to the phrase "you guys," as it was perceived as sexist. The person who brought up the objection asked how people would feel if instead the common reference was "you girls" or "you ladies." The issue of gender-inclusive language comes up a lot. Using "he" or "him" when we don't know the gender identity of the individual or others on the team can erode a sense of belonging. For example, **nonbinary** refers to individuals who do not identify as male or female and may use **gender-neutral/inclusive pronouns** such as "they" to refer to themselves.[6] Inclusive practices include not asking about gender on application forms, using "they" when one's gender is unknown, and developing a style guide for communications that incorporates gender-neutral language.

In answer to the question are we being too politically correct, I ask, What is the alternative, political incorrectness? I don't think minding our words is about political correctness. It is about equity and inclusion. The term "political correctness" has a negative connotation in today's culture. If someone accuses you of being too politically correct, you can respond with "There is nothing political about this. It is about correctness and it is about inclusion." Even if you might feel that someone is being too sensitive, it is important to self-reflect about why it bothers you and to listen empathetically to their position. Ask yourself, "How does it harm me to respect the wishes of the other person?"

Words Matter on Social Media

Given today's ever-present and often contentious social media environment, it's hard to believe that just ten years ago, social media barely existed. Social media is rampant with hurtful, hateful, demeaning, exclusive language. Words on social media can be just as abusive as words spoken face-to-face. Avoid nasty, mean, polarizing posts on social media. These are not inclusive conversations. Engage the @GoodnessBot, which is a Twitter site that promotes positivity. "Whenever you see a rude or abusive tweet, simply reply to it with @ GoodnessBot and I'll magically turn it into a positive tweet. Ta-da! Just like that you've made Twitter a kinder place." The Winters Group is using the hashtag #actsofinclusion to post stories on Twitter about people and groups who embody inclusion principles.

As discussed in Chapter 7, we live in a cancel culture. If I don't like what you said, I will rip you apart on social media and hope my post goes viral, so that millions can weigh in and cosign my opinion and maybe it will lead to your punishment and public demise. President Obama criticized the "callout" cancel culture, concerned about the trend "among young people particularly on college campuses "there is this sense that 'the way of me making change is to be as judgmental as possible about other people and that's enough.' That's not activism. That's not bringing about change. If all you're doing is casting stones, you're probably not going to get that far. That's easy to do."[7] This perpetuates the binary that there are either good people *or* bad people. People who are right *or* people who are wrong. The problem with that thinking is that DEI is messy, complex, and there are few either/ors. This is a very polarizing approach and does not support inclusive conversations.

Guidance for Inclusive
Conversations on Social Media

> **Be self-aware of your triggers.** If you see something on social media that is vehemently opposed to your core beliefs, you should pause, take a deep breath, and ask yourself why that was such a trigger for you. Do you really want to respond without reflecting some more? Is it worth it for your voice to be heard on this topic?

> **Think about the power of your words.** Are you an influencer in your field? Do you want these words to be forever etched in cyberspace? If so, think about using your power for good and to provide thoughtful and balanced commentary on social media.

> **Accept contrary opinions and be curious to learn more before attacking them.** Is there a reason to offer grace before you respond? There are boundaries. If the social media post is out of bounds (e.g., blatantly racist, sexist, etc.), you do not have to accept it, but you also do not have to respond.

> **Are you competent to respond?** There is a plethora of commentary on social media about race. Before you engage in that conversation, think about your level of competency to do so. If you are a person of color, you may be justifiably angry, but will an angry response serve the greater good? If you are white, do you know enough about the lived experiences of Black people to have a credible perspective? Are you responding from a gut reaction that might be filled with biases and prejudice based on little actual knowledge?

> **Know your why.** Are you responding just to engage in an endless debate to try to prove that you are right, and the other person is wrong? Are you trying to add a thoughtful perspective that is designed to support others' understanding, make them reflect on their own worldview? Are you trying to reach some common ground to make it possible to have an inclusive conversation about your differences?

Inclusive conversations happen when we are intentional about our word choices. This requires us to learn about those who are culturally different, their histories and preferences. While we can ask for grace and forgiveness for our faux pas, inclusion requires us to take responsibility for our own learning. If we have to spend inordinate amounts of time explaining and teaching, we slow the process to equitable actions.

SUMMARY

> Words matter.
> Microaggressions are commonplace for historically marginalized groups, and the compounding impact can be devastating.
> There are three major types of microaggressions: microassaults, microinsults, and microinvalidations.
> Microinvalidations range from gaslighting to mansplaining, whitesplaining, and distancing behaviors.
> Social media has become a venue for exclusionary, negative, and demeaning posts. A cancel culture fuels polarization and makes inclusive conversations impossible.

Discussion/Reflection Questions

1. Have a candid conversation with your team/colleagues about microaggressions and how they might be present in your organization.

2. Develop norms to mitigate microaggressions in your work or school setting. For example, Use the oops, ouch, educate model to point out microaggressions.

3. Discuss definitions. How do you define "diversity," "inclusion," "belonging," and "equity"? Is there a shared understanding of these terms?

4. How can you contribute to using social media to promote inclusive conversations?

5. Are there boundaries to inclusion? Can you be too sensitive about words, phrases, or references? How do you know if a response is "too sensitive"? Who gets to decide?

6. What are your thoughts about political correctness? Why does the term have a negative connotation? What can you do to reverse that?

From Conversation to Action

Ultimately we want to take inclusive conversations to inclusive actions that eradicate the vast societal inequities that persist. We have not mastered the ability to understand the key issues that divide us by race, ethnicity, nationality, gender, gender identity, religion, politics, and age, among other dimensions of difference, because we don't talk about them. We don't know how to talk about them, as the examples in the book show. Very rarely are the conditions necessary for success present. The conditions that I have laid out throughout this book are interconnected.

Examining oneself is paramount to any progress we can hope to make in creating a more equitable world. Using metacognitive skills invites us each to think about what we are thinking and to think before we speak. We can avoid damaging words that perhaps we did not mean that might be misinterpreted by the receiver. Self-awareness enhances our capability to understand how we differ from others, the unearned privilege that we might hold that gives us the ability to address our assumptions and biases. We cannot create brave and psychological safe spaces absent critical self-examination that engenders the capacity for trust and empathy.

By creating these key conditions, we are poised to engage in bold, inclusive conversations with those who are different in ways that lead to concerted actions for change. If you follow these recommendations, described in detail throughout the book, there is a good chance of achieving the shared goal of a more inclusive, equitable, and empathetic world.

> Acknowledge and discuss the conditions for inclusive conversations at the outset. Admit those conditions that might be missing and propose how to develop them.

> Engage in inclusive conversations for the ultimate purpose of taking action to mitigate systemic inequities.

> Engage in inclusive conversations with children. They are very impacted by world events that engender fear.

> Own your identities. We do not live in a "raceless," "postracial," or cultureless world. Like it or not, the world has classified you as a certain race and it matters. Understand how your intersecting identities influence the tone, tenor, and outcomes of conversations.

> Talk with yourself. Get to know who you are, your values, beliefs, preferences, and most important, understand why you believe what you believe.

> Recognize your own fragility, how it shows up and ways to manage it to have inclusive conversations.

> Acknowledge your power and privilege and use them to advance inclusion.

> Commit to do your part to eradicate injustices as a part of our collective responsibility.

> Develop very specific inclusive behaviors to which you will hold yourself and others accountable.

> Take responsibility for your own learning about the histories of different cultures. Don't put the burden on those from historically marginalized groups to be the teacher. It is exhausting.

> Don't minimize, or worse dismiss, other people's lived experiences that may be very different than your own.

> Extend grace and forgiveness with accountability for diversity, equity, and inclusion missteps.

> Do not endorse or engage in conversations that criticize political correctness. Such criticisms are often a way of minimizing, marginalizing, or negating others' lived experiences.

> Resist participating in the cancel culture.

> Recognize signs of trauma and unplug as you need to. Self-care is critical if you are to engage effectively in DEI work, especially inclusive conversations.

GLOSSARY

Accessibility Giving equitable access to everyone along the continuum of human ability and experience. Accessibility encompasses the broader meanings of compliance and refers to how organizations make space for the characteristics that each person brings.

Affirmative action Legislation and policies that support members of disadvantaged groups, called protected classes, that have previously suffered discrimination in such areas as education, employment, or housing. Taking affirmative action means that the organization will set goals to correct inequities in their systems that have systemically disadvantaged the protected groups based on race, gender, age, religion, nationality, color, creed, and in some states sexual orientation.

African American A person of African descent born in the United States (see also **Black**).

Agency The thoughts and actions taken by people to express their power to shape their experiences.

Allies/allyship People who uses their privilege to advocate on behalf of someone else who doesn't hold that same privilege.

Asian American A person of Asian descent born in the United States.

Baby boomer Someone born between 1946 and 1964.

Belonging Sense of psychological safety leading to the ability to be one's authentic self without fear of judgment.

Black A person having origins in any of the Black racial groups of Africa, not necessarily only in the United States. Often in the United States, all people with brown or black skin color are considered African American. However, those who are not born in the United States may identify more with their country of origin, such as Kenya or Nigeria, or as Afro-Caribbean.

Brave space/zone A condition that allows for the surfacing and sharing of each other's deep truths without fear of retribution.

Cancel culture Refers to social media. A person is ejected from influence or fame due to questionable actions or posts. It is caused by a critical mass of people who are quick to judge and slow to question.

Cisgender Denoting or relating to a person whose sense of personal identity and gender corresponds with their birth sex.

Code-shifting Act of purposefully modifying your behavior in different settings to fit the dominant cultural norm.

Collective responsibility A concept that individuals are responsible for other people's actions by tolerating, ignoring, or harboring them, without actively collaborating in these actions.

Collectivist culture Cultures that prioritize group needs over individual needs.

Covering The act of concealing something about yourself to avoid making other people feel uncomfortable or to lessen attention to a given characteristic.

Cultural misappropriation Behaving or acting in ways that represent a culture you are not a part of and interpreted as demeaning by that culture.

Decentering the dominant narrative Learning to be interested in and to talk about what something means for someone in a subordinated position based on their identity rather than always starting from framing the conversation from what something means for the dominant, normative group's perspective.

Distancing language Statements that distance one from the need/ability to take personal action.

Diversity A mix of differences in any particular setting to include but not necessarily limited to race, religion, ethnicity, gender, sexual orientation, nationality, age or generation, and job function.

Dominant group A group with systemic power, privileges, and social status within a society.

Equity The process by which we achieve fairness, equality, and inclusion that includes reallocation of resources and implementation of policies and structures that work to eliminate historical, systemic disadvantage.

Ethnocentrism An evaluation of other cultures according to preconceptions originating in the standards and customs of one's own culture.

Forgiveness To stop feeling angry or resentful toward someone for an offense, flaw, or mistake.

Gaslighting Psychological manipulation toward a historically marginalized group to make the receivers feel that the situation is their fault.

Gender Attitudes, feelings, and behaviors that a given culture associates with a person's biological sex.

Gender identity One's sense of oneself as male, female, or something else

Gender neutral/inclusive pronouns Pronouns that do not associate a gender with the individual who is being discussed.

Grace Extending kindness to the unworthy.

Imposter syndrome Feelings of inadequacy or incompetence despite demonstrated evidence of success.

Inclusion An environment where people feel valued and respected for their uniqueness and feel a sense of belonging.

Inclusive conversations Dialogue between two or more people of different cultural backgrounds (e.g., race, ethnicity, religion, gender, gender identity, ability status, and so on) for the purpose of fostering understanding about the other's culture and lived experiences for the ultimate purpose of achieving equitable outcomes.

Individualistic culture Prioritizes personal independence more than interdependence—is individually rather than group focused.

Intercultural Development Inventory A psychometric cross-cultural assessment tool that measures individual and group intercultural competence.

Internalized oppression The acceptance and adoption of negative messages about your identity group.

Intersectionality Acknowledgment that multiple power dynamics ("isms") are operating simultaneously—often in complex and compounding ways—and must be considered together to have a more complete understanding of oppression and ways to transform it.

Latinx A gender-neutral neologism, sometimes used instead of "Latino" or "Latina" to refer to people of a Latin American cultural group.

LGBTQ The acronym for lesbian, gay, bisexual, transgender, and queer or questioning.

Liberation Removing the barriers and inequities in the social systems that oppress or marginalize specific groups of people who share common identities.

Mansplaining When a man explains something to a woman in a condescending way when he either (1) doesn't know anything about it, or (2) knows far less than the woman.

Marginalized A person or group whose public or private status has been lowered through hateful, deceitful, or misguided speech or action.

Microaffirmations Subtle acknowledgments of a person's value and accomplishments that create a sense of belonging.

Microaggressions Brief, sometimes subtle, everyday comments that either consciously or unconsciously disparage others based on their personal characteristics or perceived group membership.

Microassaults Conscious, deliberate, and either subtle or explicit biased attitudes, beliefs, or behaviors that are communicated to marginalized groups through verbalizations or behaviors.

Microinequities Small, sometimes unspoken, often unconscious messages we send and receive that have a powerful impact on our interactions with others. Some common examples include a wink of understanding from across the table, or a distracted glance at the ceiling or watch while someone is speaking, or consistently mispronouncing someone's name.

Microinsults Interpersonal communications that convey stereotypes, rudeness, and insensitivity and that demean a person's identity. Unlike microassaults, microinsults are often committed unconsciously and may seem more subtle.

Microinvalidations Communications cues that exclude, negate, or nullify the thoughts, feelings, or experiential realities of certain groups.

Millennial Someone born between 1980 and 2000.

Minimization An orientation on the intercultural development continuum where one's worldview is to overemphasize similarities. This orientation is where individuals will claim to be color-blind or gender-blind and they will assert that they treat everyone the same.

Multipartiality An empathetic openness to and the ability to integrate opposing perspectives and models in dialogue.

Native American A member of any of the indigenous peoples of the Western hemisphere especially.

Nonbinary People whose gender is not male or female. Some people don't identify with any gender. Some people's gender changes over time.

Oppression Social oppression is a concept that describes the relationship between two categories of people in which one benefits from the systematic abuse and exploitation of the other.

Oppression Olympics When two or more groups compete to prove themselves more oppressed than each other.

Othering Processes and structures that engender marginality and persistent inequality based on group identities.

Perpetration Induced Traumatic Stress (PITS) Incidents of PTSD resulting from the trauma of having committed an act of violence oneself.

Political correctness The avoidance of forms of expression or action that are perceived to exclude, marginalize, or insult groups of people who are socially disadvantaged or discriminated against.

Populism A political approach that strives to appeal to ordinary people who feel that their concerns are disregarded by established elite groups.

Power System and group access, advantage, and privilege ascribed to one based on the identity groups to which one belongs.

Privilege Unearned access to resources in society and power that is only readily available to some as a result of their social group membership

Psychological safety Being able to show and employ one's self without fear of negative consequences of self-image, status, or career.

Race A social construct with little biological meaning that separates people by physical characteristics, primarily skin color.

Racism A system of advantages based on race, involving cultural messages and institutional policies and practices as well as the beliefs and actions of individuals.

Self-esteem How a person feels about herself or himself; pride in oneself. Self-esteem is linked to family traditions, language, social customs, economic background, and other aspects of one's cultural environment.

Social group identity One's sense of identity based on group membership(s)—specifically those groups that influence any given social context.

Stigmatized identities Attributes or conditions that are socially devalued and negatively stereotyped.

Subordinated group A group that has been traditionally and historically oppressed, excluded, or disadvantaged in society.

Systemic power Group access, advantage, and privilege ascribed to one based on the identity groups to which one belongs.

Systems of inequity A structurally imbalanced system that lacks equity across all groups.

Tone policing A way of invalidating concerns because of the way (the tone) in which the message was delivered. Tone policing dismisses the "issue" (e.g., the inequity, injustice, oppression, and impact it has) and centers the way in which the issue was communicated (e.g., "You sounded angry" or "You sounded divisive").

Trigger Something that forces you to relive a trauma.

Trust The sense that you can count on someone to have your best interests in mind. Trust is built by developing meaningful relationships with others.

White fragility The range of emotions (from fear, guilt, emotional distress, discomfort, defensiveness, etc.) experienced by white people when confronted with information about racial inequality and injustice.

Whiteness theory The idea that whiteness is the default of American culture, and as a result of this default, white people cannot see the advantages and disadvantages of being white due to a lack of "cultural subjectiveness" toward whiteness.

Whitesplaining Someone from a dominant group explaining to audiences of color the true nature of racism.

Woke Being conscious of racial discrimination in society and other forms of oppression and injustice. In mainstream use, "woke" can more generally describe someone or something as being "with it."

NOTES

Chapter One
What Are Inclusive Conversations and Why Are They Important?

1. T. Agovino, "Toxic Workplace Cultures Are Costing Employers Billions," Society for Human Resource Management, September 26, 2019, https://www.shrm.org/resourcesandtools/hr-topics/employee -relations/pages/toxic-workplace-cultures-are-costing-employers -billions.aspx, accessed October 3, 2019.

2. Q. Fottrell and J. Settembre, "In the #MeToo Era, 60% of Male Managers Say They're Scared of Being Alone with Women at Work," June 16, 2019, https://www.marketwatch.com/story/men-are-afraid-to -mentor-female-colleagues-in-the-metoo-era-heres-what-not-to-do -2019-05-20, accessed January 13, 2020.

3. R. Thomas, M. Cooper, E. Konar, M. Rooney, M. Noble-Tolla, A. Bohrer, and N. Robinson, "Women in the Workplace," *McKinsey & Company*, 2018, https://womenintheworkplace.com/, accessed October 1, 2019.

4. P. Thibodeau, "Employee Activism Challenges HR's Employee Experience Strategy," July 10, 2019, https://searchhrsoftware .techtarget.com/news/252466550/Employee-activism-challenges-HRs -employee-experience-strategy, accessed October 3, 2019.

5. C. Lecher, "Google Employees Protest Retaliation with International Sit-in," *The Verge*, May 1, 2019, https://www.theverge .com/2019/5/1/18525473/google-employee-sit-in-retaliation-protest, accessed October 3, 2019.

6. N. Meyersohn and K. Trafeconte, "Wayfair Workers Plan Walkout in Protest of Company's Bed Sales to Migrant Camps," CNN, June 26, 2019, https://www.cnn.com/2019/06/25/business/wayfair-walkout-detention-camps-trnd/index.html, accessed October 1, 2019.

7. J. A. Kotler, T. Z. Haider, and M. H. Levine, *Identity Matters: Parents' and Educators' Perceptions of Children's Social Identity Development* (New York: Sesame Workshop, 2019), https://www.sesameworkshop.org/what-we-do/research-and-innovation/sesame-workshop-identity-matters-study, accessed October 10, 2019.

8. A. Cooperman, "Many Americans Don't Argue about Religion—Or Even Talk about It," Pew Research, April 15, 2016, https://www.pewresearch.org/fact-tank/2016/04/15/many-americans-dont-argue-about-religion-or-even-talk-about-it/, accessed January 13, 2020.

9. Y. Shimron, "ADL Study: Violence against Jews Doubled Last Year," *Religion News*, April 30, 2019, https://religionnews.com/2019/04/30/adl-study-violence-against-jews-doubled-last-year/, accessed October 7, 2019.

10. M. Lillis, "New Zealand Mosque Killings Raise Fears among US Muslims," *The Hill*, March 15, 2019, https://thehill.com/homenews/house/434340-new-zealand-mosque-killings-raise-fears-among-us-muslims, accessed October 10, 2019.

11. J. Steele, "United Methodists Vote to Keep Traditional Marriage Stance," *Christianity Today*, February 26, 2019, https://www.christianitytoday.com/news/2019/february/united-methodist-lgbt-vote-conference-plan.html, accessed October 7, 2019.

12. L. Kaye, "December 7: A Day of Dialogue to Take Collective Action on Workplace Inclusion," *Triple Pundit*, October 9, 2018, https://www.triplepundit.com/story/2018/december-7-day-dialogue-take-collective-action-workplace-inclusion/11336, accessed October 7, 2019.

Chapter Two
Conditions for Inclusive Conversations

1. Federal Bureau of Prisons, "Inmate Race," October 5, 2019, https://www.bop.gov/about/statistics/statistics_inmate_race.jsp, accessed October 17, 2019.

2. M. Smiley, "Collective Responsibility," *Stanford Encyclopedia of Philosophy* (summer 2017), https://plato.stanford.edu/entries/collective -responsibility/, accessed October 18, 2019.

3. R. Bishop, "MLK Day: What Martin Luther King, Jr. Taught Us about Working Around Life's Obstacles," *HuffPost*, 2011, https: //www.huffpost.com/entry/mlk-day-martin-luther-king-jr-work arounds_b_809749, accessed October 18, 2019.

4. "Martin Luther King Jr. Quotes: In His Own Words," January 2018, *Birmingham Times*, https://www.birminghamtimes.com/2018 /01/some-of-dr-martin-luther-king-jr-s-profound-quotes/, accessed October 18, 2019.

5. Condé Nast Entertainment, prod., and A. Stapleton, dir., *Hello, Privilege. It's Me, Chelsea*, 2019, distributed by Netflix, https://www .netflix.com/title/80244973.

Chapter Three
First Learn How to Talk to Yourself

1. Nicolosi as quoted in R. W. Gould, "Go Ahead, Talk to Yourself. It's Normal—and Good for You," October 9, 2018, https://www .nbcnews.com/better/health/talking-yourself-normal-here-s-how -master-it-ncna918091, accessed October 29, 2019.

2. *Merriam-Webster*, "Egocentrism," https://www.merriam-web ster.com/dictionary/egocentrism, accessed October 29, 2019.

3. S. Hall, *Stuart Hall: Critical Dialogues in Cultural Studies*, edited by D. Morley and K.-H. Chen (reprint, 2005; London: Routledge, 1996).

4. A. Brookman-Byrne, "Thinking about thinking," June 22, 2018, https://bold.expert/thinking-about-thinking/?gclid=CjwKCA

jwusrtBRBmEiwAGBPgE3RTNekIlgkoCbUywCBOiruUBr9Vm
FIwch7ATN7Z3XHWZBlw2UCRkhoC3K8QAvD_BwE, accessed
October 29, 2019.

5. J. T. Jost, A. W. Kruglanski, and T. O. Nelson, "Social Meta-cognition: An Expansionist Review," *Personality and Social Psychology Review* 2, no. 2 (1998): 137–54, doi:10.1207/s15327957pspr0202_6. ISSN 1088-8683. PMID 15647141.

6. H. Tajfel and J. C. Turner, "The Social Identity Theory of Inter-group Behavior," in *Psychology of Intergroup Relations*, second edition, edited by W. G. Austin and S. Worchel, 7–27 (Chicago: Nelson-Hall, 1986).

7. M. A. Hogg and D. Abrams, "Social Motivation, Self-Esteem, and Social Identity," in *Social Identity Theory: Constructive and Critical Advances*, edited by D. Abrams and M. A. Hogg, 28–47 (New York: Harvester Wheatsheaf, 2001). J. S. Mio, L. A. Barker, and J. S. Tum-ambing, *Multicultural Psychology: Understanding Our Diverse Communities*, third edition (New York: Oxford University Press, 2012).

8. K. D. Williams, *Ostracism: The Power of Silence* (New York: Guilford Press, 2001).

9. Kimberle Crenshaw, "Demarginalizing the Intersection of Race and Sex: A Black Feminist Critique of Antidiscrimination Doctrine, Feminist Theory and Antiracist Politics," *University of Chicago Legal Forum*, no. 1 (1989): article 8, http://chicagounbound.uchicago.edu/cgi/viewcontent.cgi?article=1052&context=uclf, accessed October 20, 2019.

10. G. Corkingdale, "Overcoming Imposter Syndrome," *Harvard Business Review*, May 7, 2008, https://hbr.org/2008/05/overcoming-imposter-syndrome.

11. Emergenetics International, "What Is Emergenetics?" https://www.emergenetics.com/emergenetics-explained/, accessed March 5, 2020.

12. Institute for Health and Human Potential, "What Is Emotional Intelligence?" https://www.ihhp.com/meaning-of-emotional-intelligence, accessed October 29, 2019.

13. Intercultural Development Inventory, "The Roadmap to Intercultural Competence Using the IDI," https://idiinventory.com, accessed October 29, 2019.

14. ICS, "Resolving Conflict across Cultural Boundaries Using the Intercultural Conflict Style Inventory (ICS)," https://icsinventory .com, accessed October 29, 2019.

Chapter Four
Creating Brave, Psychologically Safe Spaces

1. M. Boykin, "An Introduction to Psychological Safety," Range, https://www.range.co/blog/introduction-to-psychological-safety, accessed January 13, 2020.

2. A. C. Edmondson and Z. Lei, "Psychological Safety: The History, Renaissance, and Future of an Interpersonal Construct," *Annual Review of Organizational Psychology and Organizational Behavior* 1, no. 1 (2014): 23–43, doi: 10.1146/annurev-orgpsych-031413-091305.

3. A. Edmonson, "Team Learning and Psychological Safety Survey," 1999, http://www.midss.org/content/team-learning-and -psychological-safety-survey, accessed October 11, 2019. A. Edmonson, "Psychological Safety and Learning Behavior in Work Teams," *Administrative Science Quarterly* 44, no. 2 (1999): 350–83, http://web .mit.edu/curhan/www/docs/Articles/15341_Readings/Group_Performance/Edmondson Psychological safety.pdf, accessed October 11, 2019.

4. L. M. Landreman, ed., *The Art of Effective Facilitation: Reflections from Social Justice Educators*, 2013, accessed October 15, 2019.

5. E. McGirt, "An Inside look at What's Keeping Black Men out of the Executive Suite," *Fortune*, January 22, 2016, https://fortune.com /longform/black-executives-men-c-suite/, accessed October 16, 2019.

6. D. R. Hekman, S. K. Johnson, M.-D. Foo, and W. Yang, "Does Diversity-Valuing Behavior Result in Diminished Performance Ratings for Non-White and Female Leaders?" *Academy of Management Journal*, March 3, 2016, https://journals.aom.org/doi/abs/10.5465/ amj.2014.0538, accessed October 15, 2019.

7. S. K. Johnson and D. R. Hekman, "Women and Minorities Are Penalized for Promoting Diversity," *Harvard Business Review*, March 23, 2016, https://hbr.org/2016/03/women-and-minorities-are-penalized-for-promoting-diversity, accessed October 15, 2019.

8. G. B. White, "Black Workers Really Do Need to Be Twice as Good," *The Atlantic*, October 7, 2015, https://www.theatlantic.com/business/archive/2015/10/why-black-workers-really-do-need-to-be-twice-as-good/409276/, accessed October 10, 2019.

9. Human Rights Campaign Foundation, "A Workplace Divided: Understanding the Climate for LGBTQ Workers Nationwide," https://assets2.hrc.org/files/assets/resources/AWorkplaceDivided-2018.pdf, accessed January 14, 2020.

10. L. Mackenzie, J. A. Wehner, and S. J. Correll, "Why Most Performance Evaluations Are Biased, and How to Fix Them," *Harvard Business Review*, January 11, 2019, https://hbr.org/2019/01/why-most-performance-evaluations-are-biased-and-how-to-fix-them, accessed January 14, 2020.

11. "Allyship," The Anti-Oppression Network, https://theantioppressionnetwork.com/allyship/, accessed October 15, 2019.

12. "Indicator 10: Bullying at School and Electronic Bullying," National Center for Education Statistics, https://nces.ed.gov/programs/crimeindicators/ind_10.asp, accessed October 9, 2019. "Suicide," National Institute of Mental Health, https://www.nimh.nih.gov/health/statistics/suicide.shtml, accessed October 7, 2019.

13. The Conscious Kid, https://www.theconsciouskid.org/about, accessed October 16, 2019.

Chapter Five
Seek Equity and Decenter Power

1. K. Putnam-Walkerly and E. Russell, "What the Heck Does 'Equity' Mean?" *Stanford Social Innovation Review*, September 15, 2016, https://ssir.org/articles/entry/what_the_heck_does_equity_mean, accessed October 10, 2019.

2. Z. Washington and L. M. Roberts, "Women of Color Get Less Support at Work: Here's How Managers Can Change That," *Harvard Business Review*, March 4, 2019, https://hbr.org/2019/03/women-of-color-get-less-support-at-work-heres-how-managers-can-change-that, accessed October 10, 2019.

3. Table 5.1 is based on Louise Diamond, "Dominant and Subordinate Group Membership," Alliance for Peacebuilding, 2014, http://www.allianceforpeacebuilding.org/wp-content/uploads/2014/06/Dominant-and-Subordinate-Group-Membership.pdf; and building on the work of Elsie Cross, *Managing Diversity: The Courage to Lead* (Westport, CT: Quorum Books, 2000).

4. "Non-Discrimination Laws," Movement Advancement Project, October 8, 2019, https://www.lgbtmap.org/equality-maps/non_discrimination_laws, accessed October 10, 2019.

5. J. Hogeveen, M. Inzlicht, and S. S. Obhi, "Power Changes How the Brain Responds to Others," *Journal of Experimental Psychology: General* 143, no. 2 (2014): 755–62, doi: 10.1037/a0033477.

Chapter Six
Face Fear and Fragility

1. K. Albrecht, "The (Only) 5 Fears We All Share," *Psychology Today*, March 2012, https://www.psychologytoday.com/us/blog/brainsnacks/201203/the-only-5-fears-we-all-share, accessed October 17, 2019.

2. K. Albrecht, *Practical Intelligence: The Art and Science of Common Sense* (New York: Wiley, 2007).

3. M. Bergmann, C. Kenney, and T. Sutton, "The Rise of Far-Right Populism Threatens Global Democracy and Security," *American Progress*, November 2, 2018, https://www.americanprogress.org/issues/security/news/2018/11/02/460498/rise-far-right-populism-threatens-global-democracy-security/, accessed October 17, 2019.

4. "Trauma," American Psychological Association, https://www.apa.org/topics/trauma/index, accessed October 10, 2019.

5. "PTSD Basics," US Department of Veterans Affairs, https://www.ptsd.va.gov/understand/what/ptsd_basics.asp, accessed October 10, 2019.

6. Quoted in *Keep Talking: Black Minds Matter—Psychological Cost of Racial Justice,* 2016, https://www.youtube.com/watch?reload=9&v=hP4Uj-vDoBA, accessed October 10, 2019.

7. S. Colino, "Fearing the Future: Pre-Traumatic Stress Reactions," *US News,* May 24, 2017, https://health.usnews.com/wellness/mind/articles/2017-05-24/fearing-the-future-pre-traumatic-stress-reactions, accessed October 10, 2019.

8. "Historical Trauma and Cultural Healing," University of Minnesota Extension, https://extension.umn.edu/mental-health/historical-trauma-and-cultural-healing#what-is-historical-trauma?-378610, accessed October 10, 2019.

9. "Perpetration Induced Traumatic Stress," Metta Center for Nonviolence, https://mettacenter.org/definitions/pits/, accessed October 10, 2019.

10. R. DiAngelo, *White Fragility: Why It's So Hard for White People to Talk about Racism* (Boston: Beacon Press, 2018).

11. S. Towey, ed., "Impact of Fear and Anxiety," University of Minnesota, https://www.takingcharge.csh.umn.edu/impact-fear-and-anxiety, accessed October 17, 2019.

12. R. DiAngelo, "White Fragility," *International Journal of Critical Pedagogy* 3, no. 3 (2011): 54–70.

Chapter Seven
Extend Grace and Forgiveness

1. "Dr. Bernice King: Weatherman Who Said 'Martin Luther Coon King' Should Not Have Been Fired," TMZ, January 10, 2019, https://www.tmz.com/2019/01/10/dr-bernice-king-weatherman-racial-slur-martin-luther-coon-fired-rehabilitation-second-chance/, accessed October 17, 2019.

2. T. Gabriel, J. Martin, and N. Fandos, "Steve King Removed from Committee Assignments over White Supremacy Remark," *New*

York Times, January 14, 2019, https://www.nytimes.com/2019/01/14/us/politics/steve-king-white-supremacy.html, accessed October 17, 2019.

3. "What Is Forgiveness?" *Greater Good Magazine*, https://greatergood.berkeley.edu/topic/forgiveness/definition, accessed January 13, 2020.

4. Harriet Kimberly Foster [For Harriet], *We Can't Cancel Everyone* [Video], June 9, 2018, https://www.youtube.com/watch?v=DOwWsvUeDFo&feature=youtu.be, accessed October 30, 2019.

5. John Hopkins Medicine, "Forgiveness: Your Health Depends on It," https://www.hopkinsmedicine.org/health/wellness-and-prevention/forgiveness-your-health-depends-on-it, accessed October 17, 2019.

6. M. Volf, *Free of Charge: Giving and Forgiving in a Culture Stripped of Grace* (Grand Rapids, MI: Zondervan, 2010).

7. D. Tutu and M. A. Tutu, *The Book of Forgiving: The Fourfold Path for Healing Ourselves and Our World*, edited by D. C. Abrams (New York: Harper-Collins, 2014).

8. J. Brankovic, "Accountability and National Reconciliation in South Africa," *Ediciones InfoJus: Derechos Humanos*, no. 4 (2013): 55–86, https://www.csvr.org.za/images/docs/Other/accountability_and_national_reconciliation_in_south_africa.pdf, accessed January 13, 2020.

9. R. Ali, "New Documentary 'Emanuel' Reveals the Power of Forgiveness after Charleston Church Massacre," *USA Today*, June 17, 2019, https://www.usatoday.com/story/life/movies/2019/06/17/emanuel-explores-power-forgiveness-after-charleston-church-massacre/1478473001/, accessed October 17, 2019.

10. J. Culver, "'I Want the Best for You': Botham Jean's Brother Hugs Amber Guyger in Emotional Courtroom Scene," *USA Today*, October 2, 2019, https://www.usatoday.com/story/news/nation/2019/10/02/amber-guyger-sentencing-botham-jeans-brother-embraces-guyger/3847967002/, accessed October 17, 2019.

11. "Man Who Survived Attack on New Zealand Mosque Says He Can Forgive Suspected Killer," CBC Radio, March 22, 2019, https://www.cbc.ca/radio/thecurrent/the-current-for-march-22-2019

-1.5066427/man-who-survived-attack-on-new-zealand-mosque-says
-he-can-forgive-suspected-killer-1.5066443, accessed October 17, 2019.

12. G. Lopez, "Ta-Nehisi Coates Has an Incredibly Clear
Explanation for Why White People Shouldn't Use the N-Word,"
Vox, November 9, 2017, https://www.vox.com/identities/2017/11/9
/16627900/ta-nehisi-coates-n-word, accessed October 30, 2019.

13. C. L. Aguilar, *Ouch! That Stereotype Hurts: Communicating
Respectfully in a Diverse World* (Bedford, TX: The Walk the Talk
Company, 2006).

Chapter Eight
Facilitate Trust and Empathy

1. D. Cox, J. Navarro-Rivera, and R. P. Jones, "Race, Religion, and
Political Affiliation of Americans' Core Social Networks," Public
Religion Research Institute, August 3, 2016, https://www.prri.org
/research/poll-race-religion-politics-americans-social-networks/,
accessed October 3, 2019.

2. "Dr Brené Brown: Empathy vs Sympathy," Twenty One Toys,
https://twentyonetoys.com/blogs/teaching-empathy/brene-brown
-empathy-vs-sympathy, accessed October 30, 2019.

3. E. McGirt, "An Inside Look at What's Keeping Black Men out
of the Executive Suite," *Fortune*, January 22, 2016, https://fortune.com
/longform/black-executives-men-c-suite/, accessed October 10, 2019.

4. B. G. White, "Black Workers Really Do Need to Be Twice as
Good," *The Atlantic*, October 7, 2015, https://www.theatlantic.com/
business/archive/2015/10/why-black-workers-really-do-need-to-be
-twice-as-good/409276/, accessed October 10, 2019.

Chapter Nine
Foster Belonging and Inclusion

1. M. Huppert, "Employees Share What Gives Them a Sense of
Belonging at Work," October 25, 2017, https://business.linkedin.com
/talent-solutions/blog/company-culture/2017/employees-share-what
-gives-them-a-sense-of-belonging-at-work, accessed October 18, 2019.

2. Quoted in K. Reilly, "How LinkedIn's HR Chief Is Changing the Diversity Conversation with 'Belonging,'" January 9, 2017, https://business.linkedin.com/talent-solutions/blog/diversity/2017/how-linkedins-hr-chief-is-changing-the-diversity-conversation-with-belonging, accessed October 18, 2019.

3. R. Thomas, M. Cooper, E. Konar, M. Rooney, M. Noble-Tolla, A. Bohrer, and N. Robinson, "Women in the Workplace," 2018, McKinsey & Company, https://womenintheworkplace.com/, accessed October 1, 2019.

4. Culture Amp, "6 Ways to Foster Belonging in the Workplace," https://hello.cultureamp.com/hubfs/1703-Belonging/Culture-Amp_6-ways-to-foster-belonging.pdf, accessed October 18, 2019.

5. C. H. Emrich, M. H. Livingston, D. H. Pruner, L. H. Oberfeld, and S. H. Page, "Creating a Culture of Mentorship," December 27, 2017, https://www.heidrick.com/Knowledge-Center/Publication/Creating_a_culture_of_mentorship, accessed October 18, 2019.

6. L. M. Shore, A. E. Randel, B. G. Chung, M. A. Dean, K. H. Ehrhart, and G. Singh, "Inclusion and Diversity in Work Groups: A Review and Model for Future Research," *Journal of Management* 37, no. 4 (2011): 1262–89, doi: 10.1177/0149206310385943, accessed October 18, 2019.

7. Figure 9.2 drawn by The Winters Group, Inc., based on content from L. M. Shore et al., "Inclusion and Diversity in Work Groups: A Review and Model for Future Research," *Journal of Management* 37 (2011), doi 10.1177/0149206310385943.

8. H. A. Krishnan and D. Park, "A Few Good Women—On Top Management Teams," *Journal of Business Research* 58 (2005): 1712–20.

9. E. Goffman, *Stigma: Notes on the Management of Spoiled Identity* (United Kingdom: Touchstone, 2009).

10. K. Yoshino, *Covering: The Hidden Assault on Our Civil Rights* (New York: Random House, 2006).

11. E. Blad, "Students' Sense of Belonging at School Is Important: It Starts with Teachers," *Education Week*, June 21, 2017, https://www.edweek.org/ew/articles/2017/06/21/belonging-at-school-starts-with-teachers.html, accessed October 18, 2019.

12. K. Legette, "School Tracking and Youth Self-Perceptions: Implications for Academic and Racial Identity," *Child Development* 89, no. 4 (2018): 1311–27.

Chapter Ten
Acknowledge and Own Whiteness

1. "Translating the Past: Inspired by Shakespeare, Race, and Colonialism and Sir John Davies 'A Discovery,'" *Early Modern British Isles Blog*, October 10, 2015, https://publish.illinois.edu/canderson /2015/10/10/translating-the-past-inspired-by-shakespeare-race-and -colonialism-and-sir-john-davies-a-discovery/.

2. DB, "Full Text of Charleston Suspect Dylann Roof's Apparent Manifesto," *TPM*, June 20, 2015, https://talkingpointsmemo.com/ muckraker/dylann-roof-manifesto-full-text, accessed October 21, 2019.

3. J. M. Horowitz, A. Brown, and K. Cox, "Race in America 2019," Pew, April 9, 2019, https://www.pewsocialtrends.org/2019/04/09/race -in-america-2019/, accessed October 21, 2019.

4. D. Hartmann, J. Gerteis, and P. R. Croll, "An Empirical Assessment of Whiteness Theory: Hidden from How Many?" *Social Problems* 56, no. 3 (2009): 403–24, doi:10.1525/sp.2009.56.3.403. JSTOR 10.1525/sp.2009.56.3.403.

5. P. McIntosh, "White Privilege: Unpacking the Invisible Knapsack," Wellesley, MA: Wellesley College Center for Research on Women, 1988, https://www.racialequitytools.org/resourcefiles/ mcintosh.pdf, accessed October 21, 2019.

6. S. Sullivan, *Good White People: The Problem with Middle-Class White Anti-Racism* (Albany: State University of New York Press, 2014), https://www.hypatiareviews.org/reviews/content/301, accessed October 21, 2019.

7. T. Jones, "The Positive Power of Whiteness?" *Inclusion Solution*, October 6, 2016, http://www.theinclusionsolution.me/a-point-of -view-the-positive-power-of-whiteness/, accessed October 21, 2019.

8. R. DiAngelo, *What Does It Mean to Be White?: Developing White Racial Literacy*, revised (New York: Peter Lang Pub, 2016).

9. A. Mansbach and K. W. Bell, "'Whites against Trump': Kamau Bell Tells White People—Yes, Even You Good Liberals—to 'Come Get Your Boy,'" *Salon*, December 15, 2015, https://www.salon.com/2015/12/15/whites_against_trump_kamau_bell_tells_white_people_yes_even_you_good_liberals_to_come_get_your_boy/, accessed October 21, 2019.

10. Jones, "Positive Power of Whiteness?"

Chapter Eleven
Mind Your Words

1. D. W. Sue, *Microaggressions in Everyday Life: Race, Gender, and Sexual Orientation* (Hoboken, NJ: Wiley, 2010).

2. C. Pierce, J. Carew, D. Pierce-Gonzalez, and D. Willis, "An Experiment in Racism: TV Commercials," in *Television and Education*, edited by C. Pierce, 62–88 (Beverly Hills, CA: Sage, 1978).

3. Pierce et al., "Experiment in Racism."

4. J. Elder and B. Iron, "Distancing Behaviors among White Groups Dealing with Racism," handout.

5. "Definitions of Diversity, Equity, Accessibility, and Inclusion," American Alliance of Museums, 2018, https://www.aam-us.org/programs/diversity-equity-accessibility-and-inclusion/facing-change-definitions/, accessed January 14, 2020.

6. "Understanding Non-Binary People: How to Be Respectful and Supportive," National Center for Transgender Equality, October 5, 2018, https://transequality.org/issues/resources/understanding-non-binary-people-how-to-be-respectful-and-supportive, accessed January 14, 2020.

7. Quoted in C. Cillizza, "What Barack Obama Gets Exactly Right about Our Toxic 'Cancel' Culture," CNN, October 30, 2019, https://www.cnn.com/2019/10/30/politics/obama-cancel-culture/index.html, accessed October 31, 2019.

INDEX

ABIDE (advancing belonging, inclusion, diversity, equity), 109, 148
Accessibility, 148
#Actsofinclusion, 151
Affirmative action, 72, 148
African American athletes, 106
African American women, hairstyles of, 117, 137–138, 140, 143, 144
African American workers, discrimination against, 50, 107
African Americans, 91–93, 134. *See also* Whitesplaining
   code-shifting and, 49
   collectivism and, 28
   and conversations shutting down when race is brought up, 104–105
   demonstrating empathy for, 103–104
   fear and anxiety, 70–71
   fragility and, 78–80
   "living while Black," 70
   microaggression against, 138, 143–144
   and the N-word, 93, 94
   power differences and interactions with whites in workplace, 60–62
   and the racial binary, 125
   racial identity, race consciousness, and, 37–38, 70–71, 124, 125, 128, 133
   religion and, 119, 126
   slavery, indentured servitude, and, 126–127
   "teaching," 144
   violence against, 13, 73, 74, 90, 103, 127
Agency, 60, 129
"Aggressiveness" and gender, 50–51
Aguilar, Leslie, 95
Albrecht, Karl, 71, 72
Allies, 15, 53
Allyship, 92, 146
   defined, 53
Anxiety. *See* Fear(s)
Apartheid, 63, 89, 90
Autonomy, fear of loss of, 71

Baby boomers, 110
Barr, Rosanne, 84, 127
Bell, W. Kamau, 130, 134

ACKNOWLEDGMENTS

I am blessed with a circle of family, friends, mentors, and colleagues who are always there to provide love, support, and encouragement—too many to name them all here. I would like to acknowledge some. First my adult children and their spouses: Dr. Joseph Winters (son), Dr. Kamilah Legette (daughter-in-law), Mareisha Reese (daughter), and Byron Reese (son-in-law). Joseph is a tenured associate professor of religion at Duke University. He specializes in critical race theory and besides being a loving son, he was a great thought partner in developing the concepts for this book. Kamilah is a research associate at the University of North Carolina, Chapel Hill. She studies the impact of racial bias in educational environments and was also a helpful thought partner. I reference some of her research in the book. Mareisha serves as chief operating officer for The Winters Group and is a daily inspiration, constantly helping me to think more clearly and practically about my ideas. Mareisha's husband, Byron, is supportive and loving and a wonderful champion of The Winters Group. He is present at all of our events helping behind to scenes to ensure our success.

I acknowledge my late partner, Kenneth Newby, who passed away on December 8, 2019. He was always there loving me and supporting my work. My extended family includes his children,

Kenton and Cicily Newby, and their children, Olivia and Savannah. We share a special bond of love that I will always cherish. Family is everything and while I cannot name everyone, I am grateful for the support of my brother, sisters-in-law, nieces, nephews, and cousins.

Every amazing member of The Winters Group team has participated in some way in the production of this book. They reviewed each chapter and provided invaluable feedback. They are:

Kevin Carter, Principal Strategist

Megan Ellinghausen, Marketing and Branding Associate

Scott Ferry, Manager, Learning and Innovation

Brittany J. Harris, Vice President, Learning and Innovation

Travis Jones, Principal Strategist

Leigh Morrison, Manager, Learning and Innovation

Krystle Nicholas, Project and Financial Analyst

Chevara Orrin, Principal Strategist

Katelyn Peterson, Public Relations and Events Coordinator

Mareisha Reese, Chief Operating Officer

Keley Smith Miller, Operations Manager

Thamara Subramanian, Manager, Learning and Innovation

Valda Valbrun, Principal Strategist

Bahiyyah Walker, Principal Strategist

I give a special shout-out to Katelyn Peterson, who was most intimately involved as research assistant and editor. As with my first Berrett-Koehler book, Steve Piersanti and many others at BK provided me with invaluable insights and kept pushing me (in caring ways) to be more succinct! I acknowledge the support of my special circle of friends, including Marcia Fugate, Tina DaCosta, Gail Livingston, Odaris Jordan, Mildred Campbell, Carmen Brown, Charlotte Downing, Peggy Harvey Lee, Carol Champ, Irene Bradley, Mary Patton, Delores Geter, Marie Rivers, Brenda Caine, and Gabrielle Webster.

Finally, I acknowledge all of the diversity, inclusion, equity, and social justice practitioners who work tirelessly every day in pursuit of justice for all, especially the "Diversity Divas," with whom I daily share my joys, successes, frustrations, and disappointments that come with this work.

ABOUT THE AUTHOR

Mary-Frances Winters came of age during the civil rights movement of the 1960s. Starting with her days as editor of her high school newspaper, Winters realized that diversity, equity, and inclusion work is her "passion and calling." Founding The Winters Group was the next step in fulfilling what she believes is her true purpose on this earth—breaking down barriers and building bridges across differences. As CEO of The Winters Group for the past thirty-six years, Winters has been able to magnify the impact of her thought-provoking message and has gained extensive experience in working with senior leadership teams to drive organizational change.

Among her many awards and distinctions, Winters received the Winds of Change award, conferred by the University of St. Thomas at the Forum on Workplace Inclusion, for her efforts to change lives, organizations, and communities. She has served as a torch bearer for the Olympics and has previously been recognized as an ATHENA Leadership Award winner from the

Chamber of Commerce for her professional excellence and for actively assisting women in their attainment of professional excellence. Winters received the Hutchinson Medal from her alma mater, the University of Rochester, in recognition of outstanding achievement and notable service to the community, state, or nation. She has also been recognized as a diversity pioneer by *Profiles in Diversity Journal* and named by *Forbes* as one of the top ten trailblazers in diversity and inclusion.

Winters is a life member of the Board of Trustees of the University of Rochester and has served on the boards of the Chamber of Commerce, United Way, and the National Board of Girl Scouts of the USA. She is the author of four other books: *We Can't Talk about That at Work!: How to Talk about Race, Religion, Politics, and Other Polarizing Topics; Only Wet Babies Like Change: Workplace Wisdom for Baby Boomers; Inclusion Starts with "I"; and CEOs Who Get It: Diversity Leadership from the Heart and Soul.* She also wrote a chapter in the book *Diversity at Work: The Practice of Inclusion* and numerous articles.

Winters has impacted hundreds of organizations and thousands of individuals that often describe her as thoughtful, credible, results-oriented, and innovative. She is known as a provocateur, especially in sharing the importance of Bold, Inclusive Conversations® that was developed to encourage organizations to create brave spaces and have dialogue around difficult workplace conversation topics such as race, religion, and politics.

ABOUT THE WINTERS GROUP, INC.

The Winters Group, Inc. is a certified minority- and women-owned global diversity and inclusion consulting firm headquartered in Charlotte, North Carolina. For more than three decades, The Winters Group has supported leaders and organizations, large and small, with developing transformative, sustainable solutions for equity and inclusion. The Winters Group has partnered with hundreds of organizations to develop, execute, and measure strategies that foster inclusion and lead to breakthrough results.

The Winters Group envisions a world that values, respects, and leverages our similarities and differences. Some of The Winters Group's unique offerings include:

> Diversity, Equity and Inclusion Strategy Development
> Cultural Audits (Surveys, Focus Groups, Interviews)
> Learning and Education
> Change Management
> Executive Coaching
> Keynote Speaking and Conference Facilitation
> Engaging in Bold, Inclusive Conversations Certification
> Fostering Cultural Competence Certification

> Understanding Identity and Building Bridges
> Mapping the Intersection of Inclusion and Social Justice
> Radical Inclusion Certification
> Em*POWER*ment Institute
> Cracking the Code of Unconscious Bias
> Diversity, Equity, Inclusion Facilitator Institute Certification

Since its inception in 2018, The Winters Group corporate social responsibility arm, Live Inclusively Actualized, has given $125,000 in grants to 501(c)3 organizations dedicated to breaking down systemic barriers for marginalized women and youth.

Also by Mary-Frances Winters

We Can't Talk about That at Work!

How to Talk about Race, Religion, Politics, and Other Polarizing Topics

Conversations about taboo topics happen at work every day. And if they aren't handled effectively, they can become polarizing and divisive, impacting productivity, engagement, retention, and employees' sense of safety in the workplace. In this concise and powerful book, Mary-Frances Winters shows how to deal with sensitive subjects in a way that brings people together instead of driving them apart. She helps you become aware of the role culture plays in shaping people's perceptions, habits, and communication styles and gives detailed guidance for structuring conversations about those things we're not supposed to talk about.

Paperback, ISBN 978-1-5230-9426-4
PDF ebook, ISBN 978-1-5230-9427-1
ePub ebook ISBN 978-1-5230-9428-8
Digital audio, ISBN 978-1-5230-9425-7

Berrett–Koehler Publishers, Inc.
www.bkconnection.com   **800.929.2929**

Dear reader,

Thank you for picking up this book and welcome to the worldwide BK community! You're joining a special group of people who have come together to create positive change in their lives, organizations, and communities.

What's BK all about?

Our mission is to connect people and ideas to create a world that works for all.

Why? Our communities, organizations, and lives get bogged down by old paradigms of self-interest, exclusion, hierarchy, and privilege. But we believe that can change. That's why we seek the leading experts on these challenges—and share their actionable ideas with you.

A welcome gift

To help you get started, we'd like to offer you a **free copy** of one of our bestselling ebooks:

www.bkconnection.com/welcome

When you claim your **free ebook**, you'll also be subscribed to our blog.

Our freshest insights

Access the best new tools and ideas for leaders at all levels on our blog at ideas.bkconnection.com.

Sincerely,

Your friends at Berrett-Koehler